Vegetarian

Baby & Child

Recipes and Practical Advice
for Raising a Healthy Child

Petra Jackson

CRESCENT BOOKS
New York • Avenel

This 1995 edition published by Crescent Books,
distributed by Random House Value Publishing, Inc.
40 Engelhard Avenue, Avenel, New Jersey 07001

Random House
New York · Toronto · London · Sydney · Auckland

ISBN 0-517-12152-2

This book was designed and produced by
Quarto Inc
6 Blundell Street
London N7 9BH

Senior editor Kate Kirby
Designer Julie Francis
Text editor Deborah Savage
Picture researcher Susannah Jayes
Illustrator Jane Strother
Photographer Laura Wickenden
Picture research manager Giulia Hetherington
Editorial director Mark Dartford
Art director Moira Clinch

Typeset in Great Britain by Central Southern Typesetters, Eastbourne
Manufactured in Hong Kong by Regent Publishing Services Ltd
Printed in China by Leefung-Asco Printers Ltd

CONTENTS

Introduction

*T*here has never been a more gratifying time to raise your precious baby on a healthy diet without meat. Hardly a week goes by without a report from a scientific source recommending that we should cut back on our consumption of animal produce, and correspondingly increase the amount of fresh fruit, vegetables, whole grains and pulses we eat. Vegetarians have been doing just that for years.

Why be a vegetarian?

The reasons for becoming a vegetarian are as individual and numerous as the vegetarian population, which, according to World statistics, is growing annually in the west by roughly 17%. Becoming more health-conscious is one of the main reasons quoted for embracing vegetarianism; when you consider that most of the animals reared for eating are fed on an alarming cocktail of hormones, antibiotics and other chemicals, whose long-term effects on animal and human aren't known, it is not surprising that we don't want our children exposed to these unnecessary dangers. Can it be coincidence that childhood disorders, such as eczema, asthma and psoriasis, appear to have increased in parallel with increasingly high levels of meat consumption?

Equally important, why should we inflict misery and suffering on animals purely in the name of profit and eating pleasure? Ecologically, there are sound reasons to be a vegetarian. Since the end of the second world war we have destroyed over 40% of the tropical rain forests to lay down grass plains for raising beef cattle. This is madness when you consider that, compared to the huge amount of plant stuff eaten by animals, only 10% ends up on our plates. It makes more sense to forget the cows and eat the plants ourselves.

There are other advantages to raising your child as a vegetarian. A decade or two ago it would have been considered odd, but, thankfully, the health message is slowly dripping through and a vegetarian diet is now something to aspire to rather than despise.

The time when being a non-meat-eater can become a little tricky is when your children become older; you tend to have less control of their eating habits. Birthday parties used to be the first minefields, with the ubiquitous hamburger; nowadays, with more mothers working, it may be your day care provider whom you will need to advise of your little one's dietary preferences. The best way to get round this is to find a like-minded carer, or to arrange to provide all your baby's food yourself. At parties and other social events where meat is likely to be served, tell the parents of the party-giver. In these enlightened times it is unlikely that your child will be the only vegetarian in the group.

What is a vegetarian?

Vegetarians fall into three main groups:

Vegans Vegans eat only plant-based foods, and no dairy products, eggs, milk, etc.

Strict Vegetarians Strict vegetarians do not eat any animal, or animal-based product if the animal was killed for the purpose, but they do eat some dairy products, such as eggs, milk and yogurt and rennet-free cheese (labeled vegetarian cheese).

Lacto-vegetarians Lacto-vegetarians simply don't eat dead animals. The lacto-vegetarian diet tends to be unique to the individual: most will eat dairy products, though some will eat only vegetarian cheese, and will certainly not touch lard or gelatin (the gelling agent derived from rendered animal bones). It is towards this latter group that this book is aimed. You may also have heard of people calling themselves "demi-vegetarians," who eat fish and white meat, but this book concentrates on the needs of lacto-vegetarians.

Your child's nutritional requirements

Overleaf is a chart outlining the six essential nutrients required for a healthy human. Here you can discover the role of each nutrient in maintaining the body and the best food sources of each. The recommended daily allowances of each nutrient will vary according to the baby's age and sex. It is important to remember that a growing baby's nutritional needs are as individual as the baby – what may be satisfying for one child might be starvation for another. More simply, the wider the variety of foods your child enjoys, the more certain you can be that he or she is receiving a balanced diet.

To help you judge what is a balanced diet, foods can be classified into five main groups. Aim to give your child at least one serving from each group every day.

Every food provides energy, which is measured in kilocalories (kcal), popularly known as just "calories." As your baby grows, energy requirements dramatically increase. As well as the same balance of nutrients (protein, carbohydrate, fat, vitamins, minerals and dietary fiber) more food is needed to fuel all that growing. Compared with adults, babies have surprisingly high energy needs: 1,900 calories for a woman; 865 for a one-year-old girl rising to 1,545 calories at 4–6 years.

Your baby's appetite will be the best indicator of how much food to give. As with adults, this will vary from day to day, or week to week and, remember, an emerging new tooth or a cold may affect appetite.

Achieving a balanced diet for your baby is easy if you allow at least one serving from each of these five different groups every day.

Group 1
Pulses, eggs, tofu and nuts

Group 2
Milk, yogurt, cheese and other milk products

Group 3
Cereals, bread, flour, rice and pasta

Group 4
Vegetable fats, oils, margarine and butter

Group 5
Fresh fruit and vegetables

Six essential nutrients for health

Protein

Protein is needed for growth and for healing. Any extra is used as energy. Protein is made up of 12 essential amino-acids. Soya is the only plant-based food that contains all the amino-acids, but cheese and other dairy products do contain them all. Other vegetarian foods – nuts, seeds, grains and pulses – are still good sources of protein but don't contain all the amino-acids.

Fats

Fats are required for energy; fat-stores help the young baby to maintain body heat. Foods that contain fat also include the fat-soluble vitamins, A, D, E and K, which is why it is important that babies drink whole milk (full-fat milk), for at least their first three years.

Carbohydrate

Carbohydrate is the body's main source of energy. It comes in two forms: starches and sugars. There are refined and unrefined versions.

Refined sugars are found in soft drinks, cakes and cookies; natural sources are fruits, vegetables, and fruit juices. Refined starches are found in white flour, bread, rice and pasta, as well as processed breakfast cereals. Unrefined starches are found in potatoes, pulses and dried beans, whole grain cereals, bread and flour. In both cases it is the natural, unrefined sources that are the best choice for nutrition and health.

Vitamins

Vitamins are essential for growth and for the healthy maintenance of the body. There are two types: fat-soluble and water-soluble.

Water-soluble vitamins, that is the B group and vitamin C, cannot be stored in the body, so it is important that you feed your baby foods containing these every day. These vitamins are easily dissolved in water and destroyed by heat; so take care, when preparing foods rich in Vitamin C, not to overcook them or to leave them immersed in water for any length of time.

The fat-soluble vitamins are vitamins A, D, E, and K.

It is unusual for children in developed countries to require vitamin supplements if they eat a balanced diet. However, because vitamins are essential for development of the brain and central nervous system, parents of vegetarian – and more particularly vegan – children should discuss this matter with their doctor or paediatrician.

The primary importance of each vitamin is as follows:

Vitamin A promotes growth, and healthy skin and teeth enamel, and good eyesight.
Sources: apricots, whole milk and eggs, carrots, oranges, tomatoes, dark-green vegetables, margarine, lentils.

Vitamin B group, confusingly, covers a large number of different B vitamins. They are necessary aids for digestion, for maintaining a healthy nervous system and for changing food into energy.
Sources: B-group vitamins are found together in many foods, but a vegetarian's main complete source is yeast extract. Other sources include: eggs, whole grain cereals, bananas, potatoes, nuts and dried beans.

Vitamin C is essential for growth and healing and it must be present if the body is to absorb iron properly.
Sources: this vitamin is found in all fruit and vegetables; the best sources are citrus fruit, kiwi fruit, blackcurrants, cranberries, strawberries, tomatoes, green vegetables, peppers, potatoes, cauliflower.

Vitamin D works with calcium to create healthy bones and teeth.
Sources: oils, eggs, margarine.

Vitamin E is necessary for the composition of body cells. It also helps to maintain and create new red blood cells.
Sources: vegetable oils, margarine, nuts.

Vitamin K aids blood-clotting and helps maintain the skeleton.
Sources: whole grain cereals, most vegetables.

Minerals

Calcium and iron are the two essential minerals. Calcium is needed for strong bones and teeth; iron for healthy blood-cells and muscle growth. Calcium-rich foods are milk and cheese, dried fruit, bread, flour, pulses and some green vegetables. Iron is mainly found in egg-yolks, whole grain cereals, green leafy vegetables and chocolate.

Water

Babies are more at risk from dehydrating than adults. It is vital that you maintain your baby's fluid levels with regular drinks. In the first weeks of life, most babies, particularly those who are breast-fed, need no more than their regular feeds. However, in hot weather, or when traveling, a supply of cooled, freshly boiled water will help quench your baby's thirst.

Food allergies

The main point to remember on this subject is that food allergies are very rare. Unless there is a family history of food allergies, there is no reason to suppose your baby will suffer. Moreover, as babies' immune systems are not fully matured, a food that causes a reaction in one month may prove harmless a month or two later. If you introduce foods one at a time you will reduce the risk of a reaction, and can identify the culprit easily, if there is a reaction.

The main symptoms of an allergic reaction are:

- vomiting (some babies vomit more than others anyway, but you can probably tell if vomiting is more serious than usual);
- vomiting coupled with diarrhea;
- diarrhea;
- rash (from pale pink to deeper colored blotches);
- swelling;
- continual crying (again, you can probably judge if your baby is crying more than usual);
- baby draws its knees up and cries.

If you believe your baby has an allergy, or are at all worried about feeding or are in any doubt of your child's well-being, never feel afraid to consult your doctor. Babies can fall ill very quickly, and vomiting and diarrhea will dehydrate them rapidly, so always call in the experts.

Always listen to and follow the expert advice you get from your doctor, pediatrician or dietitian. They will know what is best. Don't try to diagnose or treat the baby yourself.

Common food allergies

Gluten Gluten is the protein found in wheat, barley, oats, and rye. Sensitivity to gluten can lead to coeliac disease, which is why doctors recommend that all babies follow a gluten-free diet in the first year.

Cow's milk protein A baby sensitive to cow's milk protein will be prescribed a modified, soya-based milk. Breast-feeding mothers of babies with this sensitivity should perhaps cut down on their dairy intake, if advised by a doctor, as the protein they eat can be transferred to the baby.

Lactose intolerance Lactose is a milk sugar. Infants who suffer from an intolerance to it do not have an allergy in the true sense: rather, they lack the enzyme lactase, which is needed for breaking down lactose into simple sugars. Moreover, some children who are lactose-intolerant can happily eat other dairy products.

Eggs A very few babies are allergic to eggs. In addition, though not an allergy, the problem of salmonella contamination in raw or undercooked eggs needs to be considered. Guidelines are that you can give hard-cooked egg-yolks after eight months and similarly cooked egg-whites and whole eggs after a year.

Planning and freezing meals

You will see that the chapters in this book are divided by age group, starting from when you first start to wean your baby through to the toddler and then school age. At the end of each chapter there is a four-week menu planner, to help you choose your child's meals. There are quite a few choices but, in reality, you will most frequently repeat the recipes your child enjoys most. This is where your freezer will come in handy. By the age of 9–10 months your baby will probably be eating the same meals as the family. An easy and efficient way to feed them is to prepare and freeze baby-size portions of whatever you are cooking. Each recipe states whether it is suitable for freezing. You may like to prepare and freeze double batches of certain foods, particularly cookies, bread and pastry cases.

Freezing baby foods

When you are preparing purées for your baby, it makes sense to make more than you need and freeze the remainder. If you do this every time you cook, you'll save yourself a lot of time and work. You'll soon build up a stock of meals for when time is short, leaving you more time to enjoy being with your child.

You will need a freezer that can freeze food to 0° F and your containers must be sterile. In the early days, when you need only a small quantity, ice-cube trays are ideal. When you need larger helpings, use rigid, plastic, sealable freezer containers or freezerproof dishes. When your baby is around eight months old and crawling, you no longer need to sterilize the dishes.

Three steps to success

1 Sterilize the ice-cube trays by whichever method you normally use (see page 20).
2 Cook and purée the food as described in the recipe. Cover it with a clean dish towel, or plastic wrap, but do not allow these to touch the food. Leave in a cool place (not the refrigerator) until completely cold. Using a sterilized spoon, divide the purée between the ice-cube tray sections and freeze until hard (about two hours).
3 Release the frozen cubes into new freezer bags. Seal and label the bags and keep them in the freezer for up to a month. Thaw individual portions in a loosely covered, sterilized dish. Reheat the food thoroughly in a saucepan of simmering water and let it cool to a suitable temperature before serving.

Only freeze freshly prepared foods; *never* freeze uneaten portions.

The vegetarian kitchen and pantry

When you have a family to feed, you need to organize yourself, which means keeping a store of basic ingredients. If you have both a refrigerator and a freezer of a reasonable size, you shouldn't have to go shopping for fresh foods every day.

Buying food for a young baby is easy, because they eat only small quantities of a limited number of foods but, as time goes on, you will need to extend your storecupboard. Here is a list of the essentials for a growing family. Use it as a guide the next time you go shopping. Bear in mind that some items will only be available in season; the vegetarian diet makes the most of the pleasures of choosing food that is at its very best and freshest at the time you buy it.

Fresh foods

It is better to give your baby fresh rather than processed foods. Fruit and vegetables are the obvious first candidates. Choose good-quality items. But be penny-wise with your purchases too; remember that fresh produce spoils and deteriorates fast, so if you can you may prefer to shop at a local market, where you can buy little and often.

Dried foods

These can be classified into four main groups and include long-life storecupboard basics, such as flour, rice and cereals. These are items that you can add to your shelves on each shopping trip. Buying just one item from each group will ensure your storecupboard is well stocked. Frozen foods are another kind of storecupboard item, and will enable you to take advantage of fresh seasonal purchases.

Fruits Puréed apple and mashed banana are probably the first fruit your baby will enjoy. Apples are a good source of vitamin C, while bananas are rich in potassium and fiber.

Starches The sources of these, such as bread, pasta, rice and so on, add bulk as well as protein and minerals to a baby's diet. Wholemeal varieties have a higher nutritional value.

Vegetables With so many different vegetables to choose from, a meat-free diet need never be boring. Potatoes and other root vegetables are rich in vitamins A and C and cook to a splendid purée, perfect for babies' first tastes.

Dairy Children will benefit from this concentrated source of protein, calcium, energy in the form of fats, as well as the fat-soluble vitamins D and E. Cartons of fruit yogurt make great instant puddings.

Miscellaneous There is an enormous variety of fresh fruit juice in the shops: diluted for babies, they make great thirst-quenchers.

Groceries These form the backbone of any storecupboard and comprise the usual essentials, such as dried fruits, nuts, seeds, honey, sugar, herbs and spices. Ingredients like these can enhance even the most mundane dishes. Keep in sealed containers away from direct light.

Cans and Condiments Items such as canned pulses and beans, tomatoes, and soft fruits along with prepared sauces, oils and vinegar are essential storecupboard items. Their long

shelf life means that shopping for these can be done in bulk, often saving you time and money.

Babies

4 - 8 MONTHS

*F*or the first six months of your baby's life, milk will be the principal nourishment. Breast milk contains all the six essential nutrients your baby needs (see Six Essential Nutrients for Health, page 10), while formula milk, which can be based on cow's or soya milk, will be ready-fortified with vitamins and minerals.

Your guide to weaning

When to start?

There are no hard and fast rules about when you should begin introducing your baby to solid foods. But remember that a baby's system is not capable of digesting anything other than milk in its first weeks of life, and that starting on solids too soon may result in food intolerance or allergies later.

Opinions on timing differ: some say you should start solids when the baby is of a certain weight, around 16 lb., or at 20 weeks old. Generally, your baby will let you know when it is time. Good indications are if the baby is restless and unsettled during the night, if the intervals between each feeding shorten over a prolonged period or the baby starts putting a hand (or anything else within reach) into its mouth.

What should it be?

Nature must be on the vegetarian side, because, to begin with, all babies are vegetarian. The first foods to offer are those that can be ground down to a pulp, making vegetables and fruit the ideal candidates, but there is no reason not to try cereal.

Start by offering one food only, such as puréed potato or apple. Give this for a couple of days before trying something new. In this way, if your baby does have an adverse reaction, you will know the likely culprit. Then work up to combining foods. During this time, remember not to cut down on milk feedings.

How much to give?

You will probably find that your baby will only take in about a teaspoon or two of purée at the beginning. Allow about 1 tablespoon, or 1 ice-cube portion taken from an ice-cube tray (see page 13).

One lump or two?

It is mainly with their mouths that babies find out about the world: their chief experience is oral and so it naturally follows that the texture of food is very important to them. At the beginning, purées should be very soft and wet, almost liquid. You will probably have to thin some of them with baby milk, diluted fruit juice or freshly boiled water. As your baby gets used to thicker textures, you can reduce the amount of liquid. Mashing, grating or finely chopping food encourages chewing as the baby gets older and starts teething.

Food can be cooked more lightly, fruit can be offered raw, and, after about eight months, your baby can be given rice cakes, bread, raw carrots and so on, to hold and suck.

A baby's first dinner service and cutlery set needn't be extensive; babies prefer familiar objects, so a set of each should be sufficient. Opt for those made from unbreakable melamine, available in lots of designs.

What to use?

There is no need to buy your baby a special dinner service! Tiny portions need only tiny feeding bowls, so any small dishes that can be sterilized will be fine; I suggest starting off using the top of a feeding bottle. Progress to a ramekin dish. Try to use the same style of spoon for every food: babies learn most about their world through their mouths, and it is best to keep to a familiar object. Shallow, plastic weaning spoons are best. Look for entertainingly shaped ones such as airplanes or trains. Accompanied by the right sound effects, these can liven up mealtimes and encourage eating.

For an older baby, jolly colored melamine bowls and dishes can help make meal times more fun. Again, it's not necessary to have a whole range, as babies often like to have their favorite dish all the time. Two bowls, plates and dishes should be ample. Spoons often have a habit of disappearing, however, so it's a good idea to start off with at least six.

How to start?

Make up the food in readiness. It is a good idea to have it at the same temperature as you would baby milk, but as long as it is not too hot it shouldn't matter.

Put the food into a small, sterilized dish.

Lunch time is usually a good time to begin. Give your baby a partial milk feeding first to satisfy immediate hunger. A screaming, hungry baby will not be receptive to new ideas!

Hold your baby in the normal feeding position. Use a bib to catch spills and you may find it a good idea to cover yourself too. Choose a small, shallow plastic spoon and away you go.

Establishing a routine

Try to feed your baby at the same time every day. Put everything that you need nearby before you start. Tying the bib round your baby's neck is a sure signal that it's feeding time. Babies of six months or more, who are able to sit in a high chair, can be given an empty bowl and spoon to play with while you prepare their meals. They sometimes like a companion to share mealtimes – try a favorite teddy or soft toy. (Protect these from spills with a bib of their own.) Babies like to exert their independence from a startlingly early age, so as soon as they start grabbing for the spoon, let them try to hold it themselves. Trying to copy you is common – let your baby try to feed you or teddy and don't worry about the mess. Protect the floor with newspaper or a trash bag that you can just scoop up and discard afterwards.

For some reason, you can never have enough bibs. Choose the soft, absorbent, brightly colored cotton terry-toweling type.

What if you have problems?

Don't be anxious or hurt if your baby won't eat at first. Leave it and try again the next day, or in a couple of days' time. In the very early days, milk will still be the main form of nourishment for your baby. The aim of feeding solids, at first, is to encourage the use of the muscles of the mouth, and co-ordination of the tongue and throat, by swallowing thicker-textured substances, and to begin introducing your baby to the idea of mealtimes. The best way to show them that eating can be enjoyable is to let them join in family mealtimes as soon

as possible; if necessary, bring forward your family meal, so the baby can be part of it.

If you do have several refusals, try going straight to fairly wet solid food rather than starting with milk to take the edge off the baby's appetite. Offer milk afterwards. The main thing is to avoid making a fuss and stay relaxed yourself. You can't bribe a young baby to eat: they don't understand.

Preparing food for your baby

Equipment

In the beginning you don't need elaborate food-preparation equipment. As your baby is only eating tiny quantities, a sterilized strainer and spoon are all that is required to purée food. When your baby starts to eat more, it may be worth buying a blender or food processor. Hand-held blenders are particularly good, because they can cope with varying amounts of food and will prove useful for some time to come. However when using a blender or food processor you will still have to strain some foods to get rid of any tough fibers or pips.

A steamer is also a worthwhile investment. Choose a multi-tiered type, which will allow you to cook several different dishes at the same time. Initially, you can get by with a heatproof strainer covered with a lid or foil and set over a pan of simmering water.

Whisks and blenders reduce the effort of preparing liquidized food.

Cooking

Young babies need almost all their foods to be cooked if they are to digest them easily. By far the best cooking method is steaming, but boiling, stewing or baking can all be used.

Wash the fruit or vegetable of your choice, peel, pit or seed it as appropriate, and then chop it in evenly-sized pieces. Cook the fruit and vegetable in a steamer. Or place the food in a saucepan and just cover it with cold water; bring the water to a boil and simmer for about 10 minutes, or as stated in the recipe.

Sterilizing

Hygiene is of the utmost importance. All bottles, feeding cups, spoons and so on should be washed and sterilized. Once your baby is mobile, and starts to investigate the world via what it can put in its mouth, you can relax a bit about sterilizing the feeding things. Milk bottles and nipples should still be sterilized for up to a year, however.

Boiling Utensils should be completely immersed in boiling water for 5 minutes. Remove them with tongs and let them dry quickly in the air.

Steaming A cabinet specifically designed to take baby bottles, nipples and other utensils is the best method for steaming. A timer and thermostat incorporated in the machine ensures that the correct time and temperature for sterilizing is set.

Menu planner
Your four-week baby mealtime guide

	Early morning	Late morning	Lunch	Afternoon	Snack	Bedtime
Week 1						
Days 1–7	milk	milk	puréed vegetable	milk	puréed fruit	milk
Week 2						
Same as week 1						
Week 3						
Days 1 & 2	milk	milk	Vegetable Duo	milk	Orchard Purée	milk
Days 3 & 4	milk	milk	Vegetable Trio	milk	Banana Rice	milk
Days 5 & 6	milk	milk	Risotto	milk	Fruit Creams	milk
Day 7	milk & banana	milk	Baked Sweet Potato	milk	Peach Cake	milk
Week 4						
Day 1	milk & banana	milk	Baked Pumpkin with Orange	milk	Cauliflower Fluff	milk
Day 2	milk & banana	milk	Cream of Vegetables; Dried-Fruit Compote	milk	Tropical Dream	milk
Day 3	milk & pear	milk	Poached Parsley Mushrooms	milk	Tomatoes and Tofu	milk
Day 4	milk & pear	milk	Lentil and Tomato Medley; Passion Pudding	milk	Pom-Poms	milk
Day 5	milk & apple	milk	Baked Beet and Potato; Rice Pudding	milk	Fruit Cream	milk
Day 6	milk & apple	milk	Vegetable Quartet; Apricot Condé	milk	Fruit Cream	milk
Day 7	milk & peach	milk	Risotto; Dutch Apple	milk	Teeny Tahini	milk

Puréeing

Making purées couldn't be simpler. Drain the cooked fruit or vegetable and allow it to cool for a few minutes. Push it through a strainer or blend it until it is completely smooth. Add a little of the cooking water or baby milk to adjust the consistency.

Use this menu planner (above) as a guide, but if your baby prefers one dish to another, offer this on several occasions. Don't make lots of work for yourself planning new meals every day. At snack time offer a separate drink: try diluted fruit juice or cooled, freshly boiled water.

LUNCHES

A variety of easy-to-prepare nutritious savory purées to get your baby started on the right track. Don't be too concerned if your baby doesn't appear interested at first. Babies have a naturally sweet tooth (breast milk is very sweet) and new flavors will take getting used to.

MAKES: *5 portions*
PREPARATION TIME: *10 minutes*
COOKING TIME: *15 minutes*
FREEZING: *recommended*

INGREDIENTS
4 oz potato, peeled and cut in small cubes
baby milk

HINTS AND TIPS

If you are baking potatoes for the family, bake one for your baby too. Preheat the oven to 400°F. Scrub the potatoes well and prick them all over. Bake for 1 hour. Halve the potatoes, scrape out the flesh with a clean teaspoon and then continue from step 3, above.

Potato purée

Puréed potatoes are a good choice of food to start your baby eating solids. They contain quite a lot of vitamin C and provide an excellent bland base that you can combine with other flavors as your baby becomes used to a wider range.

1 Put the potato cubes in a small saucepan and pour in enough cold water just to cover them.
2 Bring the water to a boil, cover the pan and simmer for 10–15 minutes, or until the potatoes are tender. Drain well.
3 Mash the potatoes with enough baby milk to give a smooth paste. Press the paste through a sterilized strainer. Add more baby milk if necessary to obtain a thick, slightly runny consistency.

Vegetable duos

Other root vegetables, such as carrot, rutabaga, and parsnip, can be easy partners for potatoes. They can be prepared and cooked together, saving you time and effort.

1 Put the cubed vegetables in a small saucepan and pour in enough water just to cover them. Bring the water to a boil, cover the pan and simmer for 10–15 minutes, or until the vegetables are tender. Drain well.

2 Mash the vegetables with baby milk to a smooth paste. Press the paste through a sterilized strainer and add more baby milk if necessary, to obtain a thick, slightly runny consistency.

MAKES: *10 portions*
PREPARATION TIME: *10 minutes*
COOKING TIME: *15 minutes*
FREEZING: *recommended*

INGREDIENTS
4 oz potato, peeled and cut in small cubes
4 oz carrot, parsnip or rutabaga, peeled and cut in small cubes
baby milk

Vegetable trio

Combine the starchy root vegetable with tomatoes for a lighter alternative. Once skinned and seeded, tomatoes are easily digested; although they contain a lot of water they are a good source of vitamins A and C.

1 Put the cubed vegetables in a small saucepan. Pour in enough water just to cover them.

2 Bring the water to a boil, cover the pan and simmer for 10–15 minutes, or until the vegetables are tender.

3 Meanwhile, put the tomato into a small bowl and pour over enough boiling water to cover it. Leave for 30 seconds. Drain and rinse under cold running water and carefully rub away the skin.

4 Drain the potato and carrot when they are cooked. Halve the tomato, remove the core and scoop out all the seeds. Chop the flesh very finely and then mash it with the cooked vegetables and baby milk to a smooth paste. Press the paste through a sterilized strainer, adding more milk if necessary, to obtain a slightly runny paste.

MAKES: *10 portions*
PREPARATION TIME: *15 minutes*
COOKING TIME: *15 minutes*
FREEZING: *recommended*

INGREDIENTS
4 oz potato, peeled and cut into small cubes
4 oz carrot, peeled and cut into small cubes
1 firm, ripe tomato
baby milk

MAKES: *12 portions*
PREPARATION TIME: *15 minutes*
COOKING TIME: *20 minutes*
FREEZING: *recommended*

INGREDIENTS

2 oz white part of leek
4 oz potato, peeled
4 oz rutabaga, peeled
*1 firm, ripe tomato, skinned and
   seeded*
*1¼ cups vegetable stock (see page
   138)*

Vegetable quartet

*As feeding progresses, combine new flavors with those that your
baby has already become familiar with. Leeks have a sweeter,
milder flavor than onions; they can be introduced when your baby
is about 5 months old.*

1 Carefully wash the leek to remove all soil, then trim and slice
finely. Cut the potato and rutabaga in small cubes. Put all the
prepared vegetables in a small saucepan and add the stock.
2 Bring the stock to a boil, cover the pan and simmer for 15–20
minutes, or until the vegetables are tender. Purée the vegetables
with the stock until smooth. Allow to cool slightly before serving.

MAKES: *about 12 portions*
PREPARATION TIME: *20 minutes*
COOKING TIME: *varies according to
   vegetable used*
FREEZING: *not recommended*

INGREDIENTS

*4 oz zucchini, green beans, broccoli,
   or spinach*
*half a gluten-, salt- and sugar-free
   zwieback*
¾ cup baby milk
2–3 teaspoons freshly boiled water

Cream of vegetables

*In this recipe, vegetables are combined with a small salt- and
sugar-free zwieback and baby milk to provide a more substantial
purée than one using just vegetables. This is particularly suitable
for the more watery vegetables. As your baby gets older, make the
cream thicker by reducing the amount of liquid you add at the end
of step 4.*

1 Prepare your vegetables: trim and slice zucchini or beans; divide
broccoli into small flowerets; remove any tough stalks from spinach.
Rinse well and drain.
2 Steam the vegetables for 10–15 minutes (5–10 minutes for spinach),
or until tender.
3 Meanwhile, crumble the zwieback into a small dish and warm the
baby milk. Mix together to form a smooth paste.
4 Purée the vegetables with the freshly boiled water until smooth.
Strain if necessary. Stir into the milk mixture and mix with more
baby milk or boiled water to obtain a smooth, thick runny consistency.

> **HINTS AND TIPS**
> *A similar cream can be prepared
> using 2–3 teaspoons of commercial
> baby rice in place of the zwieback.
> Check the package for ingredients
> and instructions.*

Baked sweet potato

Sweet potatoes have a delicious flavor that babies love. They are a great source of carbohydrate, vitamins and minerals and can be baked or boiled. Parsnip is an excellent partner for sweet potato.

1 Preheat the oven to 400°F. Cook the vegetables on a baking sheet for about 1 hour or until tender.
2 Halve the sweet potato and, using a teaspoon, scoop out the flesh and put it in a bowl with the parsnip.
3 Mash with baby milk until soft and smooth. Press through a strainer, if necessary, and then stir in the coriander.

MAKES: *6 portions*
PREPARATION TIME: *15 minutes*
COOKING TIME: *1 hour*
FREEZING: *recommended*

INGREDIENTS
6 oz sweet potato, scrubbed
4 oz parsnip, trimmed and peeled
baby milk
a tiny pinch of ground coriander

Baked pumpkin with orange

A classic combination of flavors, which can be adapted to suit your baby's taste. If possible, use a freshly squeezed orange for the maximum flavor and nutritional benefit.

1 Preheat the oven to 375°F. Lightly oil a 7-inch square of foil. Put the pumpkin in the center of the foil and lift up each corner to form a cup. Pour the orange juice over the pumpkin and dot with the margarine. Sprinkle with sugar.
2 Twist the corners of foil to seal the parcel and then set it on a baking sheet. Cook for 1½ hours, or until the pumpkin is tender.
3 Scoop out the flesh and purée it with the cooking juices until smooth. Allow to cool a little, if necessary, before serving.

MAKES: *6 portions*
PREPARATION TIME: *15 minutes*
COOKING TIME: *1½ hours*
FREEZING: *recommended*

INGREDIENTS
6 oz fresh pumpkin, skinned and
  seeded
1 small orange, squeezed
1 tablespoon soya margarine
a pinch of light turbinado sugar

Four-season risottos

As the name suggests, this recipe uses seasonal vegetables to provide your baby with the best of the crop. Fresh young spring vegetables, sun-ripened summer crops, autumn harvest vegetables, and winter roots provide varying amounts of vitamins A, B, and C, calcium and iron.

EACH RECIPE MAKES: *12 portions*
PREPARATION TIME: *up to 20 minutes*
COOKING TIME: *up to 20 minutes*
FREEZING: *not recommended*

INGREDIENTS
FOR ALL THE RISOTTOS:
2 tablespoons unsalted cooked white rice
Baby milk
FOR THE SPRING RISOTTO:
2 oz each young carrots and new potatoes, trimmed, peeled and roughly chopped
4 oz fresh young spinach leaves, washed and roughly shredded
FOR THE SUMMER RISOTTO:
2 oz each zucchini and sweet red pepper
1 firm ripe tomato, skinned and seeded
FOR THE AUTUMN RISOTTO:
2 oz each cauliflower flowerets, okra and potato
FOR THE WINTER RISOTTO:
2 oz each rutabaga, turnip and parsnip, trimmed, peeled and cubed

1 For the spring risotto, cook the carrot and potato in boiling water for 15 minutes, or until tender. Add the spinach to the water 3 minutes before the end of the cooking time. Drain well.

For the summer risotto, trim the zucchini and chop it roughly. Peel the pepper and remove any seeds and fibrous parts. Chop it roughly with the tomato. Steam the vegetables for 10 minutes or until tender.

For the autumn risotto, trim the okra and peel the potato. Cook with the cauliflower in boiling water for 15 minutes, or until tender. Drain well.

For the winter risotto, cook the vegetables in boiling water for 20 minutes, or until tender. Drain well.

2 Purée the vegetables with the rice and enough milk to give a smooth, soft consistency. Push through a sterilized strainer, if necessary.

Lentil and tomato medley

Lentils are a good source of protein, but should only be combined with vegetables in small proportions for very young babies.

1 Put the lentils in a saucepan and pour in enough cold water to cover by about ½ inch. Bring to a boil, skim any froth from the surface and simmer for 5 minutes. Drain and return to pan.
2 Roughly chop the tomatoes and add them to the lentils, with the tomato juice. Bring to a boil, cover and simmer gently for 25–30 minutes, stirring frequently, until the lentils are very soft. Strain before serving, and allow to cool a little, if necessary.

MAKES: *6 portions*
PREPARATION TIME: *25 minutes*
COOKING TIME: *35 minutes*
FREEZING: *not recommended*

INGREDIENTS
3 tablespoons red lentils
4 firm, ripe tomatoes, skinned and seeded
½ cup tomato juice

Poached parsley mushrooms

Choose fresh, open-cup mushrooms and ensure they are wiped thoroughly before poaching them. There is no need to wash or peel mushrooms as long as trapped dirt is carefully wiped away.

1 Poach the mushrooms with the parsley in the baby milk over a low heat for 10–15 minutes, or until tender. Take care that the milk doesn't catch on the base of the pan.
2 Purée to a smooth, soft consistency. Add more milk and allow to cool a little, if necessary.

MAKES: *4 portions*
PREPARATION TIME: *10 minutes*
COOKING TIME: *15 minutes*
FREEZING: *not recommended*

INGREDIENTS
4 oz mushrooms, stalks removed, sliced
1 tablespoon chopped fresh parsley
about ½ cup baby milk

Baked beets and potato

Beets make a colorful meal and provides a fair amount of vitamin B as well as calcium. Buy raw beets rather than ready-cooked ones, because the latter are often soaked in brine.

1 Preheat the oven to 325°F. Remove any whiskery threads from the beets; don't pierce the skin, or it will leak during cooking. Place the vegetables in a small dish and cover with foil.
2 Cook for 2 hours, or until the vegetables are tender and the beets skin will rub away easily.
3 Halve the potato and scoop out the flesh. Purée it with the beets and baby milk.

MAKES: *6 portions*
PREPARATION TIME: *10 minutes*
COOKING TIME: *2 hours*
FREEZING: *not recommended*

INGREDIENTS
4 oz baby beets
6 oz potato, scrubbed and pricked
baby milk

SUPPER

More easy-to-prepare purées, both sweet and savory, to tempt your baby with. Try to balance the combination of foods you offer your baby in one day. If your baby has had a fairly robust lunch, offer a light fruit purée at suppertime. See the suggested menu on page 21 as a guide.

MAKES: *6 portions*
PREPARATION TIME: *15 minutes*
COOKING TIME: *5 minutes*
FREEZING: *not recommended*

INGREDIENTS
2 eating apples, peeled, cored and chopped
1 dessert pear, peeled, cored and chopped
1 ripe plum, skinned and pitted
3 tablespoons apple juice

Three-fruit purée

At the height of their season (early–mid September), plums will be at their sweetest. For young babies they may have a purging effect, so offer only a little, mixed with other fruits. Skin the plum in the same way as you would a tomato.

1 Put the apple and pear into a saucepan with the apple juice and 3 tablespoons water. Bring to a boil.
2 Add the plum and simmer gently for 5 minutes, or until softened. Purée until smooth. Adjust the consistency with freshly boiled water and allow to cool before serving.

Orchard purée

Puréed apples and pears are ideal fruit for babies; on first taste they may be a little tart, however. If your baby isn't tempted, try combining orchard fruit with sweeter fruit such as mashed banana or, when in season, fresh plums (see Three Fruit Purée, opposite).

1 Put the fruit and apple juice in a small saucepan with 3 tablespoons water. Bring to a boil.
2 Cook over a medium heat for 10 minutes, stirring occasionally, until the fruit is tender. Cool slightly and then purée the fruit. Adjust the consistency with freshly boiled water.

MAKES: *4 portions*
PREPARATION TIME: *15 minutes*
COOKING TIME: *10 minutes*
FREEZING: *recommended*

INGREDIENTS
1 medium-size eating apple, peeled, cored and chopped
1 medium-size dessert pear, peeled, cored and chopped
3 tablespoons pure apple juice

Tomatoes and tofu

Tofu is protein-packed and incredibly bland in flavor. Make sure you buy fresh or silken tofu, rather than the smoked or flavored kind.

1 Preheat the oven to 350°F. Lightly grease a small ramekin dish with sunflower oil.
2 Drain the tofu and purée it with the tomato and about 2 teaspoons of baby milk, until smooth. Spoon into the ramekin and cook for 15–20 minutes until risen and set.
3 Spoon into a cold dish and allow to cool for a few minutes before serving.

MAKES: *1 portion*
PREPARATION TIME: *10 minutes*
COOKING TIME: *20 minutes*
FREEZING: *not recommended*

INGREDIENTS
2 oz tofu
1 firm, ripe tomato, skinned, de-seeded and roughly chopped
baby milk

Pom-poms

Makes: *4 portions*
Preparation time: *10 minutes*
Cooking time: *1 hour*
Freezing: *recommended*

INGREDIENTS
6 oz potato, scrubbed
1 eating apple, cored
baby milk

Apple and potato is an unusual combination, but with an appealing texture and mild flavor, and lots of vitamins B and C, it's sure to be a winner.

1 Preheat the oven to 400°F. Prick the potato. Wrap the apple loosely in foil. Bake both for 1 hour or until tender.
2 Halve the potato. Using a teaspoon, scoop out the flesh from the potato and apple and purée it with baby milk. Allow to cool a little, if necessary, before serving.

Teeny tahini

Makes: *1 portion*
Preparation time: *5 minutes*
Freezing: *not recommended*

INGREDIENTS
½ small, ripe avocado
⅛ teaspoon unsalted tahini paste
baby milk, if necessary

Tahini is a paste made from sesame seeds which is used widely in Oriental and African recipes. Combined with avocado, it provides huge helpings of unsaturated fat and is a rich source of vitamins B and E.

Remove the pit from the avocado, and, using a teaspoon, scoop out the flesh. Purée it with the tahini paste until smooth. Adjust the consistency with freshly boiled water or baby milk if necessary.

Cauliflower fluff

Makes: *4 portions*
Preparation time: *15 minutes*
Cooking time: *15 minutes*
Freezing: *not recommended*

INGREDIENTS
4 oz cauliflower flowerets
3 tablespoons fine soya meal
Baby milk or freshly boiled water

The presence of soya boosts the protein in this savory. Cauliflower can be a bit strongly flavored for young babies, so it would be wise to offer this when solid feeding has become more established.

1 Steam the cauliflower flowerets for 10 minutes, or until tender. Purée them with the soya meal and baby milk or water until smooth.
2 Spoon the mixture into a small saucepan and stir it over a medium heat for 5 minutes, until slightly thickened. Adjust the consistency with more baby milk or freshly boiled water.

Banana rice

Although it's a refined product, commercial baby rice cereal is a great standby. Choose an unflavored variety and combine it with fruit purées to create your baby's favorite.

Make up the baby rice cereal with baby milk or water as directed on the package. Peel and mash the banana until smooth and then stir in the baby rice cereal. Mix them together thoroughly.

MAKES: *1 portion*
PREPARATION TIME: *5 minutes*
FREEZING: *not recommended*

INGREDIENTS
1 tablespoon baby rice cereal
baby milk
1/2 banana

Banana buddies

Bananas, like potatoes, are an ideal base for a number of purées. Alone, they are the perfect convenience food, requiring little preparation and no cooking.

Mash the banana until smooth. Purée the fruit with the juice from the can. Mix into the banana.

MAKES: *1–2 portions*
PREPARATION TIME: *5 minutes*

INGREDIENTS
1/2 banana, peeled
*1 canned apricot, peach or pear half
  in natural juice*
1 tablespoon of juice from the can

HINTS AND TIPS
Other banana buddies can include puréed fresh apple, kiwi fruit, mango, and soaked dried apricots. Make only enough to use at one time, because bananas turn black if kept for any length of time once peeled.

MAKES: *6 portions*
PREPARATION TIME: *10 minutes*
COOKING TIME: *5 minutes*
FREEZING: *not recommended*

INGREDIENTS
1 fresh kiwi fruit, peach or apricot
3 tablespoons unflavored baby rice cereal
baby milk or freshly boiled water

Fruit creams

Like the recipe for Cream of Vegetables (page 24), this is suited to the more watery fruit, such as kiwi fruit, peaches or apricots. Use unflavored baby rice.

1 Peel the fruit and remove the stone or seeds as appropriate. Chop the flesh roughly and poach it in 1 tablespoon of water for 5 minutes, until tender.

2 Mix the baby rice cereal with the baby milk or water as directed on the package. Mix the rice into the fruit and then purée until smooth. Adjust the consistency with more baby milk or freshly boiled water.

Rice pudding

An easy favorite: use flaked rice for quickness and serve with a fruit purée or mashed banana for added sweetness.

1 Mix the rice and milk together in a small saucepan. Stir over a low heat for 5 minutes or until the mixture thickens and begins to boil.
2 Simmer for 5 minutes, stirring frequently. Allow to cool for a few minutes before feeding this to your baby.

MAKES: *2 portions*
PREPARATION TIME: *2 minutes*
COOKING TIME: *10 minutes*
FREEZING: *not recommended*

INGREDIENTS
1 tablespoon flaked rice
²⁄₃ cup baby milk

Tropical dream

The custard apple contributes to the soft creamy texture of this recipe, but, like the banana, it blackens on keeping – so prepare this just before you need it.

1 Poach the mango for 5 minutes with 1 tablespoon water for 5 minutes, or until tender. Purée until smooth.
2 Mash the banana. Halve the custard apple and, using a teaspoon, scoop out the flesh. Mix with the mango and banana and then purée until smooth.

MAKES: *2 portions*
PREPARATION TIME: *10 minutes*
COOKING TIME: *5 minutes*
FREEZING: *not recommended*

INGREDIENTS
½ ripe mango, peeled and roughly chopped
½ banana
1 small custard apple

Peach cake

Unsalted rice cakes may not look appealing, but they combine beautifully with soft fruit purées to create new textures and tastes for your baby to try.

1 Soak the rice cake in the peach juice until soft. Purée it with the peach until smooth.
2 Adjust the consistency with more juice or freshly boiled water.

MAKES: *4 portions*
PREPARATION TIME: *5 minutes*
FREEZING: *not recommended*

INGREDIENTS
1 unsalted rice cake
about 3 tablespoons peach juice from the can
1 canned peach in natural juice

DESSERTS

Babies do not necessarily have to have a two-course meal on every occasion, but it is nice to be able to offer your baby a variety of tastes and textures. Included here are a number of easy-to-prepare favorites, and your baby, in time, is sure to let you know which are the winners.

MAKES: *12 portions*
PREPARATION TIME: *5 minutes*
COOKING TIME: *30 minutes*
FREEZING: *recommended*

INGREDIENTS
2 oz each dried apricots, apples,
  peaches and prunes
1 dried fig
¹/₂ inch vanilla pod

Dried-fruit compote

Dried fruit has concentrated amounts of vitamins and minerals, which are unlocked during cooking. To retain as much of the goodness as possible, purèe the fruit with the cooking liquid.

1 Check the fruit for pips and stems and remove them. Chop the fruit roughly and put it into a saucepan, with the vanilla pod. Pour over enough boiling water to cover the fruit by about 1 inch.
2 Bring the water to a boil, cover the pan and simmer gently for 25–30 minutes, until tender. Remove the vanilla pod and then purée the fruit until smooth. Allow to cool a little before serving.

Dutch apples

Simple apple purée can be perked up with a few golden raisins. Their natural sweetness will offset the tart apple, as well as adding some potassium.

1 Soak the golden raisins in a little boiling water until plump. Drain them and put them in a saucepan, with the apple, cinnamon and 1 tablespoon of water.
2 Simmer, stirring frequently, for 10 minutes or until the apple is soft. Purée until smooth. Adjust the consistency with freshly boiled water, and allow to cool a little before serving.

MAKES: *2 portions*
PREPARATION TIME: *5 minutes*
COOKING TIME: *10 minutes*
FREEZING: *not recommended*

INGREDIENTS
2 teaspoons golden raisins, rinsed
1 eating apple, peeled, cored and chopped
a tiny pinch of ground cinnamon

Passion pudding

Passion fruit may seem a little exotic for a tiny baby, but the fragrant flesh of this fruit purées easily and a little goes a long way.

Using a teaspoon, scrape the flesh from the passion-fruit and strain it to remove the pips. Mash the banana until smooth and then stir in the passion fruit.

MAKES: *1 portion*
PREPARATION TIME: *5 minutes*
FREEZING: *not recommended*

INGREDIENTS
½ ripe passion fruit
½ banana

Apricot condé

Use dried, canned, or fresh apricots for this easy dessert.

Purée the apricot, with the soaking water (if used), until smooth. Cook the rice as for Rice Pudding (see page 33). Stir in the apricot purée and mix well. Allow to cool a little before serving.

MAKES: *2 portions*
PREPARATION TIME: *10 minutes*
COOKING TIME: *10 minutes*
FREEZING: *recommended*

INGREDIENTS
2 ready-to-eat dried apricots, soaked in ⅔ cup freshly boiled water, or 1 canned in its own juice, or 1 fresh apricot, peeled and pitted
3 tablespoons flaked rice or instant rice
⅔ cup baby milk

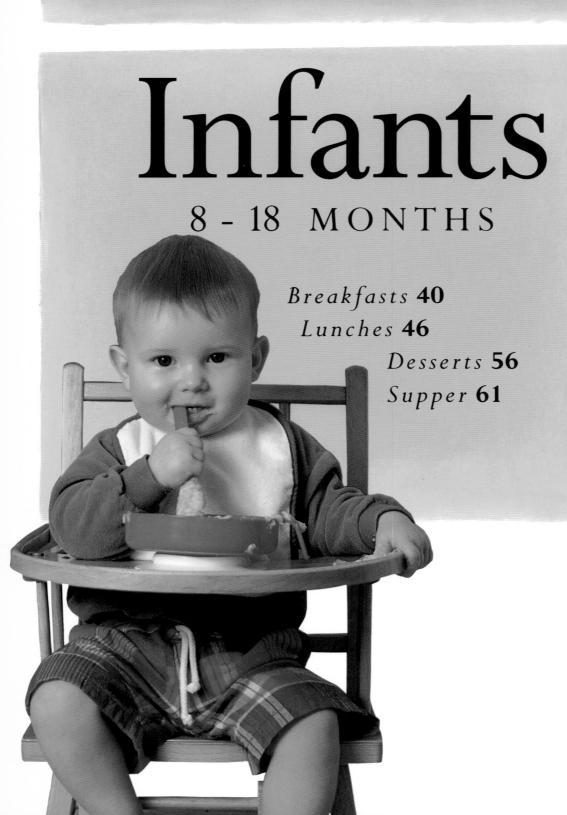

CHAPTER 2

Infants

8 - 18 MONTHS

*T*his is a period of rapid development for your baby. He or she will have
started to sit in a high chair and will no longer need to be held
during feeding. Even the younger baby will have started to cut a few teeth,
while older ones can probably chew fairly chunky foods.

Choosing utensils

Now is the time to encourage children to feed themselves and to try drinking from a cup. If you haven't yet bought any special feeding dishes, consider buying a couple of unbreakable bowls and lidded cups with spouts. Choose a cup with a close-fitting lid and a weighted base.

At this stage, most things find their way into a baby's mouth, and your previous rigid sterilizing regime becomes pointless. However, while you can ease off sterilizing bowls and spoons, you should sterilize milk-feeding bottles and nipples for up to 18 months. Bacteria can breed in the warm environment of the bottle and you must always pay special attention to cleaning the bottle and inside the nipple.

Unbreakable plastic-lidded cups, with or without handles, are the ideal containers for toddlers' drinks.

Fads and fancies

The baby won't eat lumps

For babies around eight months old, you will still need to purée food to a soft, fairly smooth consistency that toothless gums can chew. As more teeth gradually appear, you can start to make the mixture coarser.

Feeding problems often begin when you make this transition. Your baby is used to soft foods, and, though they may want to bite more, a sturdy toy or teething ring is often preferred.

Encourage chewing by providing sticks of raw vegetables, such as carrot, cucumber or celery, and start to mash food with a fork, rather than blending it in the food processor. If your baby flatly refuses to eat a coarser mixture, begin by adding some mashed or grated food to the usual purée and gradually work up to a rougher texture.

37

The baby will only eat one thing

It is surprising how a young baby can quickly adopt a fancy for one food above all others. Opinions on this problem vary: many professionals take the line that if the baby is still drinking milk and appears happy and healthy, there is no reason to make a fuss; if you ignore it they will grow out of it. Others feel that it is important to lead by example: the sight of the family enjoying mealtimes together, and eating a variety of interesting foods, will make the baby want to join in.

The baby won't eat

The leading-by-example strategy is a good one to try first. Babies are good imitators, so prepare your baby's meal as usual and eat your own meal. Make no fuss or comment if the baby refuses the food, simply take it away and try again next time.

Novelty cutters can transform ordinary foods into something more attractive for fussy eaters.

Children are very influenced by color and always seem to go for brightly colored foods first. Try to combine some contrasting colors and shapes on their plates. You may like to buy some small petit-four cutters or novelty cookie cutters in different shapes. Carrot slices and even toast looks more appealing in the shape of a flower or star.

For some reason, the food from Mom or Dad's plate seems tastier and more attractive than the baby's own. Try feeding your baby straight from your own plate for a couple of mealtimes.

For older children who won't eat, forget set mealtimes. Try packing a picnic and eat it together. You don't have to go outdoors. Try throwing an old sheet over the table and sit underneath it in a makeshift tent. Have a teddy bears' picnic or a toy party.

Let them help you prepare the meal or do some baking. Children love to roll out cookie dough and cut out fancy shapes.

Invite another child of similar age to lunch or supper; if possible, find one with a good appetite. Try not to give too much praise to the hearty eater, though, or your child may feel overshadowed rather than impressed by their companion.

Finally, remember that refusing food is really only a passing phase: unlike adults, who are conditioned into eating three meals a day, a toddler will only eat when hungry, and, as far as we know, no child has ever starved itself to death through its own stubbornness!

As the menu planner (right) shows by now your baby will be eating more and not relying on milk so much for nourishment. However, as milk contains a concentrated supply of protein and calcium it is important that you give your baby at least 1 pint daily. This can be in a variety of forms, such as from yogurt and cheese, in cooked dishes and in a bottle for a between-meals drink. As your baby grows, you will need to increase the quantities of food you give at mealtimes.

Menu planner
Your four-week infant mealtime guide

	Breakfast	Late morning	Lunch	Afternoon	Supper	Bedtime
Week 1						
Day 1	Oatmeal	milk	Cheesy-topped Tomatoes; Baked Banana	fruit yogurt; juice drink	Potato Patacakes	milk
Day 2	fruit yogurt	milk	Three-bean Hash; Honey Squares	fruit purée; milk	Mini Macaroni Cheese	milk
Day 3	Vanilla and Raisin Flakes	milk; Apple Jumbles	Pumpkin Puff; milk	Melon Cooler	Cowboy Beans	milk
Day 4	Tot's Toasts	milk	Corn Chowder; Fruity Wibble Wobble	Avocado Cream; juice drink	Buttons and Bows	milk
Day 5	Apple Bix	milk	Sunshine Saucy Pasta; Honey Squares	fruit purée; milk	Chickadee Puffs	milk
Day 6	Baby Muesli	milk	ABC Cheese; Strawberry Rice	fruit yogurt; juice drink	Couscous Salad	milk
Day 7	Cheese Brunch	milk	Dilly Dhally; Farina Pudding	fruit purée; milk	Creamed Mushrooms	milk
Week 2						
Day 1	Teddy Bear Cereal	milk	Squish Squash; Milky Wibble Wobble	fruit yogurt; juice drink	Cheese Charlotte	milk
Day 2	Apricot Granola	milk	Mix-Up Mushrooms; Baked Banana	Applejack Afternooner; milk	Creamy Herb Pasta	milk
Day 3	Fresh Fruit Yogurt	milk	Sticky Rice; Pink Coconut Ice	fruit yogurt; juice drink	Cottage Bake	milk
Day 4	Strawberry Crackles	milk	Teeny Tortilla; Orange Custard Cream	Melon Cooler; milk	Potato Patacakes	milk
Day 5	Honey-bunch Brunch	milk	Mini Minestrone; Apple Jumbles	Banana and Date Whip; juice drink	Mini Macaroni Cheese	milk
Day 6	Apple Bix; Honey Squares	milk	Vegetable Cheese Ribbons	fruit purée; milk	Creamed Mushrooms	milk
Day 7	Tot's Toasts	milk	Leek and Potato Sloop; Strawberry Rice	fruit yogurt; juice drink	Buttons and Bows	milk
Week 3						
Same as week 1						
Week 4						
Same as week 2						

BREAKFASTS

As babies get older and more mobile, they will be hungrier in the mornings. Now is the time to start introducing more substantial breakfasts. Breakfast time can be a somewhat frantic affair, if you are trying to placate a hungry baby while simultaneously attempting to prepare what they are screaming for. These recipes are fast and fuss-free, and many can even be made a day or so in advance.

MAKES: *1 portion*
PREPARATION TIME: *8 minutes*
FREEZING: *not recommended*

INGREDIENTS
1 small apple, peeled, cored and grated
1/4 cup grated mild Cheddar cheese
1 oz golden raisins
1 tablespoon yogurt
1/2 teaspoon bran flakes, crushed

Cheese brunch

Try to alternate your baby's breakfast with cereal- and fruit-based dishes occasionally. This is a nice mix of the two and couldn't be easier to prepare.

Put all the ingredients, except the bran flakes, in a blender or food processor and blend briefly. Spoon into a bowl and sprinkle over the bran flakes before serving.

HINTS AND TIPS
Cheese Brunch can be made and stored overnight.

Oatmeal

Real oatmeal has no match in my view; the natural oats combined with milk have their own sweetness. This makes oatmeal a popular breakfast for babies and it's a healthy choice, as you don't have to sweeten it. Oats are high in soluble fiber, too, so oatmeal is an ideal breakfast for you and the rest of the family.

1 Put the milk in a small saucepan and bring it to a boil. Sprinkle in the rolled oats and stir well.
2 Continue to stir over a low heat until the oatmeal is thick and creamy. Leave the oatmeal to cool for a few minutes before feeding your baby. Adjust the consistency with cold milk, if necessary, if the oatmeal is too thick.

MAKES: *1 portion*
PREPARATION TIME: *2 minutes*
COOKING TIME: *5 minutes*
FREEZING: *not recommended*

INGREDIENTS
²/₃ cup milk
1 tablespoon organic rolled oats

Teddy bear cereal

A little puréed pear provides extra vitamins, while the honey adds flavor and sweetness.

1 Put the pear in a saucepan with 2 teaspoons water. Cook over medium heat for 5 minutes, or until softened. Mash with a fork. Add the milk and bring to a boil.
2 Sprinkle in the oats and stir over low heat until thickened and creamy. Stir in the honey then allow to cool for a few minutes before feeding your baby.

MAKES: *1 portion*
PREPARATION TIME: *5 minutes*
COOKING TIME: *10 minutes*
FREEZING: *not recommended*

INGREDIENTS
1 pear, peeled, cored and chopped
²/₃ cup milk
4 teaspoons organic rolled oats
¹/₄ teaspoon clear honey

HINTS AND TIPS
Purée the pear before adding it to the teddy bear cereal if your baby is still unable to eat "bits."

MAKES: *3 portions*
PREPARATION TIME: *15 minutes +*
 overnight soaking
FREEZING: *not recommended*

INGREDIENTS
1 oz each wheatgerm and rolled oats
1/2 cup unsweetened apple, orange,
 or pineapple juice
1 teaspoon clear honey
2 oz golden raisins
1 dried peach, finely chopped
1 teaspoon sour cream

Baby muesli

A batch of this will keep for three days, stored in an airtight container in the fridge. Vary the flavor according to whatever fruit is available. Most dried fruit is suitable: try dried apricots with orange or tropical fruit juice, dried pear with apple juice, or add more vine fruits and use unsweetened grape juice. Watch out, this dish has a strange habit of disappearing when there are adults about.

1 Soak the wheatgerm and oats in the fruit juice for a couple of hours. Stir in the honey and dried fruits. Soak overnight.
2 Purée a portion in a blender or food processor for about 30 seconds. Stir in the sour cream before serving.

MAKES: *1 portion*
PREPARATION TIME: *10 minutes*
FREEZING: *not recommended*

INGREDIENTS
1 tablespoon puréed fruit
1/3 cup natural yogurt
1/4 teaspoon vanilla extract
1/4 teaspoon clear honey
1/4 teaspoon wheatgerm

Fresh fruit yogurt

Ready-prepared pots of fruit yogurt can often be an expensive and wasteful purchase if your baby doesn't like the flavor you've selected. It's easy to make your own using your baby's favorites, and these won't be laced with sugar, as ready-made ones often are.

Mix together the fruit, yogurt, vanilla extract, and honey. Spoon into a bowl and sprinkle the wheatgerm on top.

HINTS AND TIPS
For older babies, try using unpuréed fruits. Hulled and mashed strawberries or raspberries work well.

Apricot granola

Similar to muesli, granola is a mix of dried fruits, toasted nuts, and cereals. Make a batch and store it in an airtight container. Then, the night before, simply soak what you need in milk, fruit juice, or yogurt.

1 Preheat the oven to 400°F. Spread the wheatgerm, oats, bran flakes and almonds in a single layer on a baking sheet. Bake for 5 minutes. Stir well and then cook for 3 minutes more, or until the almonds are evenly golden.

2 Spoon into a bowl and leave until completely cool. Add the apricots, golden raisins, cinnamon and orange rind to the roasted mixture. Store in airtight container until needed.

3 Soak a portion in ⅔ cup liquid overnight.

4 Purée in a blender or food processor for 30 seconds before serving.

MAKES: *6 adult portions*
PREPARATION TIME: *10 minutes +*
   overnight soaking
COOKING TIME: *8 minutes*
FREEZING: *not recommended*

INGREDIENTS
3 oz wheatgerm
1½ oz each rolled oats and bran
   flakes
2 tablespoons ground almonds
2 oz ready-to-eat dried apricots,
   chopped finely
1 oz golden raisins
a pinch of ground cinnamon
Grated zest of 1 small orange

Strawberry crackles

Unsweetened commercial cereals are fortified with vitamins and minerals and can be a great standby when time is really short. Buy small sample packages if possible, and, if all else fails, the baby can always play with the box.

Finely chop the strawberries and then mash them until smooth. Mix them with the cereal and warm milk. Leave to soak for 10 minutes before feeding the baby.

MAKES: *1 portion*
PREPARATION TIME: *5 minutes +*
   10 minutes soaking
FREEZING: *not recommended*

INGREDIENTS
3 small strawberries, washed and
   hulled
¼ cup puffed rice cereal
⅔ cup warm milk

> **HINTS AND TIPS**
> *Use canned or thawed frozen fruit when strawberries are out of season. Purée it in a food processor or blender if necessary.*

MAKES: *1 portion*
PREPARATION TIME: *5 minutes*
COOKING TIME: *8 minutes*
FREEZING: *not recommended*

INGREDIENTS
*1 small dessert apple, peeled, cored,
    and chopped, or 1 cube of frozen
    apple purée, thawed*
1 zwieback or rice cake
⅔ cup milk

Apple bix

Use unsweetened zwieback or rice cakes as the basis for this simple breakfast and, if you have a batch of apple purée in the freezer, all the better. Try to remember to defrost a cube in the refrigerator overnight.

1 Put the apple in a saucepan with 2 teaspoons water and cook over a low heat for 5–6 minutes, or until softened. Mash well with a fork.
2 Crumble the zwieback or rice cake into the apple and then stir in the milk. Stir over low heat until just warmed. Spoon into a serving bowl.

MAKES: *1 portion*
PREPARATION TIME: *5 minutes +
    overnight soaking*
FREEZING: *not recommended*

INGREDIENTS
*1 tablespoon Californian sun-dried
    raisins*
¼ cup natural yogurt
1 tablespoon milk
*1 tablespoon each bran flakes and
    cornflakes*
¼ teaspoon vanilla extract

Vanilla and raisin flakes

The B vitamins play an important role in a young baby's diet; they are essential for growth and a baby is using much of the vitamin B intake to do just that. Dried fruit and whole-grain cereals are a rich source of B vitamins and a good way to include them in your baby's daily menu.

1 Mix all the ingredients together. Cover and chill overnight.
2 Purée in a food processor or blender for 30 seconds, or until smooth.

HINTS AND TIPS
This may be a little chilly for some babies to eat first thing in the morning, so spoon it into a warmed serving bowl first.

Tot's toasts

This recipe gives you two options in one. For younger babies, soak the toasts in milk to soften them, and then feed the mixture to your baby with a spoon. When your child is a little older, and has some teeth and is starting to chew, offer fingers of toast to hold and gnaw on. Try using cookie cutters to cut the toast into fun shapes, such as stars and animals instead of fingers.

1 Preheat the broiler. Spread the butter, tahini paste and peanut butter over the toasted bread to cover it completely. Sprinkle over the sesame seeds and toast until just golden.
2 Cool slightly before serving.

MAKES: *1 portion*
PREPARATION TIME: *3 minutes*
FREEZING: *not recommended*

INGREDIENTS
½ teaspoon unsalted butter or margarine
¼ teaspoon tahini paste
¼ teaspoon smooth peanut butter
1 thin slice of whole wheat bread, toasted
a pinch of sesame seeds

Honey-bunch brunch

This is the type of breakfast that slips down easily, so it is great for babies who have no teeth.

Put all the ingredients in a food processor and blend briefly until smooth.

MAKES: *1 portion*
PREPARATION TIME: *5 minutes*
FREEZING: *not recommended*

INGREDIENTS
½ banana, peeled
2 canned prunes, pitted
2 teaspoons yogurt
2 teaspoons natural cottage cheese
½ teaspoon clear honey
a pinch of grated nutmeg

HINTS AND TIPS
A variation of this is to replace the banana with avocado, and the prunes with half a canned peach. Serve both varieties soon after making or they will discolor.

LUNCHES

Now your baby is moving on from mainly milk feeds, it is essential that you maintain the correct balance of body-building and energy-giving foods. Lunch is generally considered to be a baby's main meal of the day and, in this section, protein-rich meals, based on peanuts, beans, and pulses, are featured. Combined with a sensible strategy for other meals, these ideas will ensure your baby stays well nourished.

MAKES: *4 portions*
PREPARATION TIME: *15 minutes +*
    overnight soaking
COOKING TIME: *45 minutes*
FREEZING: *recommended*

INGREDIENTS
1 oz each lima beans and garbanzo beans
2 oz green beans, trimmed and chopped
1 teaspoon sunflower oil
2 oz carrot, peeled and chopped
2 oz rutabaga, peeled and cubed
4 oz potato, peeled and cubed
1/3 cup vegetable stock

Three-bean hash

Use canned beans for speed, but you must still strain them before using to get rid of the indigestible husks.

1 Soak the lima beans and garbanzo beans in cold water overnight.
2 Drain the beans and put them in a saucepan. Cover with cold water and bring to a boil. Boil rapidly for 10 minutes.
3 Skim any froth from the surface, reduce the heat and simmer for 35 minutes. Add the green beans, carrots, rutabaga and potato to the pan and cook for another 10 minutes, or until the beans and vegetables are tender. Drain well.
4 While they are still warm, press the lima beans and garbanzo beans through a strainer into a bowl. Add the cooked vegetables and mash everything well.
5 Heat the oil in a non-stick frying pan. Add the vegetable mixture and press down well with the back of a spoon. Cook over medium heat until the underside is golden. Flip over and cook the other side.
6 Divide into 4 equal pieces. Moisten with a little vegetable stock before serving.

Cheesy-topped tomatoes

The ground almonds help to thicken this baked mixed-vegetable purée, as well as providing essential protein and vitamins.

1 Preheat the oven to 350°F. Chop the tomatoes and steam them with the carrot for 10 minutes, or until tender.
2 Blend the tomatoes and carrot in a food processor or blender, with 1 oz of the Cheddar cheese and the milk, ground almonds and herbs; don't make the purée too smooth.
3 Grease four small ramekins or ovenproof cups and spoon in the tomato mixture. Sprinkle the remaining cheese on top and bake for 15 minutes, or until golden. Cool slightly before serving.

MAKES: *4 portions*
PREPARATION TIME: *20 minutes*
COOKING TIME: *15 minutes*
FREEZING: *not recommended*

INGREDIENTS
*4 firm ripe tomatoes, skinned and
   seeded*
1 carrot, peeled and chopped
1/3 cup grated Cheddar cheese
1/2 cup milk
1/3 cup ground almonds
a pinch of dried mixed herbs

Corn chowder

This is a baby-friendly version of the classic New England recipe. The potato gives it a wonderfully comforting, thick texture, and the corn adds sweetness.

1 Melt the butter in a saucepan and cook the leek and pepper over medium heat for 5 minutes, or until softened. Add the milk, corn, potato and bay leaf and bring to a boil.
2 Reduce the heat and simmer for 10 minutes or until the potato is tender. Remove the bay leaf and either mash or blend briefly in a food processor or blender.

MAKES: *6 portions*
PREPARATION TIME: *10 minutes*
COOKING TIME: *15 minutes*
FREEZING: *recommended*

INGREDIENTS
*1 teaspoon unsalted butter or
   margarine*
*2-inch piece of leek, white part only,
   sliced*
*1/4 red pepper, seeded and finely
   chopped*
1 1/4 cups milk
4 oz frozen corn
4 oz potato, peeled and chopped
1 bay leaf

MAKES: *2 portions*
PREPARATION TIME: *10 minutes*
COOKING TIME: *30 minutes*
FREEZING: *not recommended*

INGREDIENTS
1 oz cooked mashed broccoli
1 oz cooked mashed carrot
1/3 cup cooked unsalted white rice
1 tablespoon grated Cheddar cheese
1 large egg yolk
1/2 cup milk

Vegetable pots

These can be made with cooked leftover vegetables or a selection of freshly steamed vegetables.

1 Preheat the oven to 350°F. Grease two small ramekins or oven-proof cups. Mix the vegetables and rice together with 2 teaspoons of the cheese. Stir in the egg and milk and mix everything together.
2 Spoon the mixture into dishes and cover them with foil. Put the dishes in a roasting pan and fill it with boiling water to come halfway up the pan. Transfer carefully to the oven and cook for 30 minutes, or until set. Allow to cool slightly before feeding your baby.

MAKES: *8 portions*
PREPARATION TIME: *10 minutes*
COOKING TIME: *25 minutes*
FREEZING: *not recommended*

INGREDIENTS
1 teaspoon vegetable oil
1/2 small onion, peeled and chopped
4 oz each carrot, parsnip and potato, peeled and chopped
a pinch each of ground coriander and cumin
2 oz red lentils
2 1/2 cups vegetable stock

Dilly dhally

This dish is a great source of protein and inspired by a classic Indian vegetarian recipe. It is also incredibly easy to make.

1 Heat the oil in a saucepan and fry the onion for 5 minutes, or until soft. Add the carrot, parsnip and potato. Sprinkle the spices over and cook for a further 5 minutes.
2 Stir in the lentils and stock and bring to a boil. Cover the pan and leave it to simmer, stirring occasionally, for 25 minutes, or until the lentils are tender.
3 Blend briefly in a food processor or blender until smooth.

HINTS AND TIPS
If the mixture is too thick, adjust it with water or stock. For older babies, serve with unsalted breadsticks for them to hold and dip in the dhal.

Mushroom surprise

Cabbage has quite a strong flavor, which babies can dislike; but when it is combined with a fairly bland partner such as mushrooms, babies should eat it up quite happily.

1 Put the rice in a saucepan and cover with cold water to a depth of about 1 inch. Bring the water to a boil, reduce the heat, cover the rice and let it simmer for 25 minutes.
2 Add the shredded cabbage to the saucepan and cook for 5 minutes, or until the rice and cabbage are tender.
3 Meanwhile, heat the oil in a frying pan and cook the mushrooms for 5 minutes. Stir in the tomatoes and cook for 3 minutes more.
4 Drain the rice and cabbage. Blend them in a food processor or blender with half the mushroom mixture. Spoon into the serving dish. Blend the remaining mushroom mixture with the Cheddar and spoon it on top.

MAKES: *6 portions*
PREPARATION TIME: *15 minutes*
COOKING TIME: *25 minutes*
FREEZING: *not recommended*

INGREDIENTS
¼ cup brown rice
3 oz cabbage, shredded
1 teaspoon vegetable oil
4 button mushrooms, wiped and chopped
1 tomato, skinned, seeded and chopped
⅓ cup grated Cheddar cheese

Eggplant pasta

Babies and children soon seem to form a great fondness for pasta and you couldn't wish for a more convenient food. More importantly, it has carbohydrate and protein to boost energy and growth.

1 Heat the oil in a saucepan and cook the eggplant, zucchini, pepper, corn and mushrooms for 8 minutes, or until tender.
2 Stir in the tomatoes and bring to a boil. Reduce the heat, cover and simmer for 15 minutes.
3 Add the stock to the pan and return to a boil. Add the pasta shapes and cook for 10 minutes, or until the pasta is tender.
4 Allow to cool slightly and then blend briefly in a food processor or blender.

MAKES: *4 portions*
PREPARATION TIME: *20 minutes*
COOKING TIME: *33 minutes*
FREEZING: *not recommended*

INGREDIENTS
1 teaspoon sunflower oil
2 oz each eggplant and zucchini, chopped
1 strip of red pepper, seeded and cubed
1 oz corn
1 oz button mushrooms, wiped and chopped
8 oz canned chopped tomatoes
½ cup vegetable stock
2 oz pasta shapes, e.g., bows, spirals, quills etc.

MAKES: *4 portions*
PREPARATION TIME: *15 minutes*
COOKING TIME: *25 minutes*
FREEZING: *not recommended*

INGREDIENTS
4 oz pumpkin, peeled and seeded
2 oz each carrot and rutabaga
¹/₃ cup orange juice
¹/₃ cup milk
1 large egg yolk
*1 oz toasted pumpkin seeds, finely
  ground*

Pumpkin puff

**This bakes to a wonderful rich golden color, which is very
appealing. A good amount of vitamin A comes with this, too.**

1 Preheat the oven to 350°F. Grease four small ramekins or ovenproof cups. Chop the pumpkin, carrot and rutabaga into equally
sized pieces and steam them for 10 minutes, or until they are tender.
2 Blend the vegetables with the orange juice, milk, egg, and ground
pumpkin seeds until smooth. Spoon into dishes and bake for 25
minutes, or until set. Cool slightly before serving.

HINTS AND TIPS
*Due to the amount of oil they
contain, nuts and seeds deteriorate
with age. If you don't use them
regularly, store them in airtight
containers in the freezer.*

Leek and potato sloop

Soups are a little too liquid to feed to a baby by spoon, but they should be able to manage this slightly thicker version, which contains fresh spinach leaves for iron and color.

1 Melt the butter in a saucepan and cook the leek over medium heat for 3–4 minutes, or until softened. Add the potato and the spinach to the pan, with the stock.
2 Bring the mixture to a boil, cover and simmer over a low heat for 30 minutes, stirring occasionally. Mash, or blend briefly in a blender or food processor. Allow the "sloop" to cool slightly, if necessary, and stir in the sour cream just before serving.

MAKES: *8 portions*
PREPARATION TIME: *15 minutes*
COOKING TIME: *30 minutes*
FREEZING: *not recommended*

INGREDIENTS
1 tablespoon unsalted butter
1 leek, trimmed and chopped
8 oz potato, cubed
8 oz fresh spinach leaves, shredded
1¼ cup vegetable stock
1 tablespoon sour cream

Mix-up mushrooms

Sweet and sour flavors may seem a little sophisticated for a baby's palate, but in fact they love this mild version. This is made with egg-noodles for added protein and carbohydrate.

1 Put the noodles in a shallow dish and pour over enough boiling water to cover. Leave to soak.
2 Meanwhile, heat the vegetable oil in a frying pan and stir-fry the mushrooms, carrot and pepper for 4–5 minutes, or until softened.
3 Add the pineapple, bean sprouts and tomatoes and bring to a boil. Stir in the tomato catsup.
4 Drain the noodles and briefly blend them in a food processor or blender, with the vegetable mixture, until smooth.

MAKES: *1 portion*
PREPARATION TIME: *10 minutes*
COOKING TIME: *5 minutes*
FREEZING: *not recommended*

INGREDIENTS
1 oz thread egg-noodles
1 teaspoon vegetable oil
4 button mushrooms, wiped and
  sliced
2 oz carrot, peeled and cubed
1 strip each of red and green pepper,
  seeded and chopped
2 canned pineapple chunks, chopped
1 oz fresh bean sprouts
⅓ cup canned chopped tomatoes
1 teaspoon tomato catsup

MAKES: *4 portions*
PREPARATION TIME: *10 minutes*
COOKING TIME: *1½ hours*
FREEZING: *not recommended*

INGREDIENTS
1 small butternut squash
2 oz each carrot and zucchini, cubed
1 oz corn
a pinch of grated nutmeg
a pinch of soft brown sugar
1 tablespoon unsalted butter or
*   margarine*

Squish squash

Choose small young squash with few blemishes, because older vegetables can be a little bitter. Make these when you have the oven on for baking.

1 Preheat the oven to 350°F. Halve the squash lengthwise and scoop out the seeds. Mix the vegetables, nutmeg and sugar together and then use them to fill each squash.
2 Dot the butter over each squash and then wrap them in foil. Put on a baking sheet and cook for 1½ hours, or until the vegetables and squash are tender.
3 Scoop the squash flesh from the skin and mash or blend it briefly in a blender or food processor, with the filling.

MAKES: *6 portions*
PREPARATION TIME: *15 minutes*
COOKING TIME: *20 minutes*
FREEZING: *recommended*

INGREDIENTS
1 tablespoon unsalted butter or
*   margarine*
½ small onion, peeled and chopped
1 celery stalk, washed and finely
*   chopped*
¼ each green and red pepper, seeded
*   and finely chopped*
2 oz carrot, peeled and finely
*   chopped*
4 firm ripe tomatoes, peeled, seeded
*   and chopped*
1 oz red lentils
⅔ cup vegetable stock
a pinch of dried basil
2 oz pasta shapes

Sunshine saucy pasta

A simple, full-flavored tomato sauce that goes well with pasta or baked and then mashed potatoes.

1 Melt the butter in a saucepan and add the onion and celery. Cook over a medium heat for 5 minutes, until softened. Add the pepper, carrot and tomatoes and cook for 5 minutes, stirring occasionally.
2 Stir in the lentils, stock and basil. Bring to a boil, stirring continuously. Reduce the heat, cover the pan, and simmer for 20 minutes, or until the vegetables and lentils are tender and the sauce thickened.
3 While the sauce is cooking, boil the pasta for 10 minutes, or until tender. Drain well.
4 Blend the sauce and pasta briefly in a food processor or blender.

ABC cheese

Crumbled tofu and Gruyère cheese enrich and flavor this simple dish of vegetables in a tasty sauce with a crunchy wheat-flake topping. It is sure to become a favorite.

1 Steam the vegetables for 10 minutes, or until soft.
2 Meanwhile, mix the cornstarch with 3 tablespoons of the milk, to form a smooth paste. Heat the remaining milk in a saucepan until boiling.
3 Stir the milk into the cornstarch mixture and then return it to the pan. Stir over low heat until thickened and smooth. Off the heat, crumble in the tofu and grate in half the cheese. Return the pan to the heat and stir until the cheese has melted.
4 Stir the vegetables into the cheese sauce and mash or blend them briefly in a food processor or blender. Spoon into bowls and sprinkle the remaining cheese and wheat flakes on top.

MAKES: *2 portions*
PREPARATION TIME: *10 minutes*
COOKING TIME: *10 minutes*
FREEZING: *recommended*

INGREDIENTS
2 oz eggplant, peeled and cubed
3 oz broccoli and cauliflower flowerets, chopped
1 green onion, white only, trimmed and chopped
1 teaspoon cornstarch
¾ cup milk
1 oz each tofu and Gruyère cheese
½ oz wheat flakes, crushed

Mini minestrone

I've added a few white beans to pep up the protein and provide energy; remember to strain these first for babies under nine months.

1 Heat the oil in a saucepan and fry the carrot, leek and celery for 5 minutes over medium heat until soft. Add the potato and the cabbage to the pan, with the chopped tomatoes and stock.
2 Cover the pan and bring to a boil. Reduce the heat and simmer for 20 minutes.
3 Stir in the peas, beans, tomato paste and pasta. Return to a boil, and then simmer for 10 minutes, or until the pasta and vegetables are soft.
4 Mash the vegetables or blend briefly in a food processor or blender.

MAKES: *10 portions*
PREPARATION TIME: *20 minutes*
COOKING TIME: *30 minutes*
FREEZING: *not recommended*

INGREDIENTS
1 teaspoon oil
2 oz each carrot, white of leek and celery
4 oz potato, cubed
4 oz green cabbage, shredded
6 ripe tomatoes, skinned, seeded and chopped
2½ cups vegetable stock
1 tablespoon peas
1 tablespoon canned or cooked white beans
2 teaspoons tomato paste
2 oz small pasta stars

SERVES: *2*
PREPARATION TIME: *10 minutes*
COOKING TIME: *30 minutes*
FREEZING: *not recommended*

INGREDIENTS
2 rounded tablespoons brown rice
vegetable stock
2 oz each carrot, zucchini and green
* cabbage, shredded*
1 tomato, skinned, seeded and cut in
* strips*
1/3 cup grated Swiss cheese

Vegetable cheese ribbons

This can be made from a variety of vegetables — whatever you may have at hand. But when making your own combinations, pick both starchy and leaf vegetables for the best nutritional balance.

1 Cook the brown rice in the vegetable stock for 20 minutes. Add the carrot and cook for 5 minutes more. Then stir in the zucchini and cabbage.
2 Return to a boil and simmer for 5 minutes, or until the rice and vegetables are tender.
3 Stir in the tomato and half the cheese. Blend the rice mixture briefly in a blender or food processor. Spoon it into a serving dish and sprinkle it with cheese.

MAKES: *4 portions*
PREPARATION TIME: *10 minutes*
COOKING TIME: *38 minutes*
FREEZING: *not recommended*

INGREDIENTS
2 tablespoons unsalted butter or
* margarine*
1/2 small onion, peeled and chopped
1/4 cup rice
2 oz broccoli flowerets
1 strip each of red and yellow
* pepper, seeded and chopped*
2 cups vegetable stock
1/4 teaspoon yeast extract
1 oz cashew nuts, ground
1 1/2 tablespoons grated fresh
* Parmesan cheese*

Sticky rice

Round-grain pudding rice or Italian Arborio rice are the best types to use for this. They cook down to a lovely, creamy consistency, which your baby can digest easily.

1 Melt the butter in a saucepan and cook the onion over medium heat for 5 minutes or until softened. Stir in the rice, broccoli, and peppers. Cook, stirring, for 2–3 minutes.
2 Mix together the stock and yeast extract and stir into the rice mixture. Simmer gently for 30 minutes, stirring frequently, until the mixture is thick and nearly all the liquid has been absorbed.
3 Blend briefly in blender or food processor, with the ground cashew nuts and the cheese.

Teeny tortilla

Not the rough, Mexican, floury type of tortilla, but a soft pancake speckled with parsley.

1 Put the flour in a bowl and beat in the egg yolk and milk to form a smooth batter. Stir in the parsley.

2 Heat 1 teaspoon of the oil in a non-stick frying pan. Drain off excess oil and pour in about 1 tablespoon of batter. Swirl the pan so that the mixture evenly coats the bottom.

3 Cook over medium heat for 2 minutes, or until the batter has set. Flip over and cook the other side. Repeat to make six pancakes in all. Use one pancake and freeze the remainder.

4 Mash the avocado with the chopped tomato. Spread it over one pancake and roll it up. Heat the tomato sauce and blend them briefly with the stuffed pancake. Mix in sour cream before feeding to your baby.

MAKES: *6 pancakes*
PREPARATION TIME: *5 minutes*
COOKING TIME: *15 minutes*
FREEZING: *recommended*

INGREDIENTS
½ cup all-purpose flour
1 large egg yolk
1¼ cups milk
3 tablespoons chopped fresh parsley
2 teaspoons vegetable oil
FOR THE FILLING:
½ small avocado
1 tomato, skinned, seeded and chopped
3 oz thick Italian tomato sauce (passata)
2 teaspoons sour cream

> ## HINTS AND TIPS
> *The remaining pancakes will freeze. Separate them with wax paper and seal them in a plastic bag. Freeze for up to 3 months.*

DESSERTS

A simple selection of quick desserts to help finish mealtimes with a smile. Babies who are teething may lose interest in food, so forget about desserts and offer frozen fruit segments such as apple, pear, orange, or melon instead. These are great gum-soothers, which they can suck and chew, and be nourished at the same time.

MAKES: *4 portions*
PREPARATION TIME: *10 minutes +
  chilling overnight*
FREEZING: *not recommended*

INGREDIENTS
½ teaspoon vegetarian gelatin
½ pint fruit juice or purée

Fruity wibble wobble

You can use any fresh fruit juice or purée for this, except pineapple, papaya, or kiwi fruit. This is because these fresh fruits have an enzyme that prevents setting. Puréed canned fruits work fine.

1 Pour ⅓ cup fruit juice into a small bowl and sprinkle in the gelatin. Mix well until dissolved. Stand the bowl in a saucepan of hot water and leave it until just below boiling point (the liquid should be steaming but not bubbling).
2 Stir the liquid gelatin into the fruit juice or purée and pour into molds. Chill overnight until set.

HINTS AND TIPS

Color jelly with natural food coloring pastes for more vibrant effects. To create shapes, pour jelly into a shallow dish and chill until set. Stamp out shapes with cookie cutters. Letters, numbers and animal shapes are particularly appealing.

Milky wibble wobble

Soft-fruit purées, such as raspberry or strawberry, seem to work best in this milky gelatin.

1 Hull and chop the fruit. Put into a saucepan with the sugar and water and bring to a boil. Simmer for 10 minutes or until the fruit is very soft.
2 Measure ⅓ cup of the cooking liquid into a small bowl. Sprinkle in the gelatin and stir until dissolved. Strain fruit to remove pips.
3 Blend the fruit, cooking liquid, gelatin and milk together until frothy. Pour into a serving dish and chill until set.

MAKES: *4 portions*
PREPARATION TIME: *15 minutes + overnight chilling*
FREEZING: *not recommended*

INGREDIENTS
2 oz strawberries or raspberries
1 teaspoon confectioner's sugar
⅔ cup water
½ teaspoon vegetarian gelatin
⅔ cup milk

Strawberry rice

If you can, use short-grain brown rice; it will be more nutritious, with its B vitamins still intact.

1 Put the rice, vanilla extract and milk in a saucepan and bring to just below boiling. Cover and simmer, stirring occasionally, for 30 minutes or until the milk has been absorbed and the rice is tender.
2 Stir in the strawberry purée just before serving.

MAKES: *4 portions*
PREPARATION TIME: *5 minutes*
COOKING TIME: *30 minutes*
FREEZING: *not recommended*

INGREDIENTS
2 good tablespoons short-grain brown rice
¼ teaspoon vanilla extract
1¼ cups milk
2 teaspoons low-sugar strawberry spread or fruit purée

HINTS AND TIPS
Ready-prepared fruit spreads are similar to jam or jellies but made with little or no sugar; they make a useful standby pudding. Try them with yogurt or sour cream.

Apple jumbles

The oat topping adds a new texture to soft, cooked apples for baby to try. Mix the topping in and let it soften before feeding this to younger babies.

MAKES: *2 portions*
PREPARATION TIME: *10 minutes*
COOKING TIME: *20 minutes*
FREEZING: *not recommended*

INGREDIENTS

2 dessert apples, peeled, cored and chopped
1 tablespoon apple juice
2 good tablespoons golden raisins
a pinch of ground cinnamon
¼ cup each all-purpose flour and rolled oats
2 teaspoons softened unsalted butter or margarine
natural yogurt to serve, if necessary

1 Put the apples, apple juice, golden raisins, and cinnamon in a small saucepan and cook over medium heat for 10 minutes, or until softened.
2 Meanwhile, mix together the flour, oats and butter to form a crumble. Spoon the apple mixture into two small ramekins and put the oat mixture on top. Preheat the broiler to high and toast the topping for 3–4 minutes, or until just golden.
3 Stir the oat topping into the apple mixture to combine. Allow to cool before serving. Moisten with a little yogurt if your baby finds the mixture too dry.

Honey squares

This delicious pudding makes use of an easy all-in-one cake mixture; the lemon and honey syrup makes it deliciously moist.

MAKES: *16 squares*
PREPARATION TIME: *10 minutes*
COOKING TIME: *30 minutes*
FREEZING: *recommended*

INGREDIENTS

4 tablespoons soft margarine
4·tablespoons superfine sugar
2 oz self-rising whole wheat flour
1 egg yolk
1 tablespoon milk
1 tablespoon clear honey
grated peel and juice of 1 small lemon
natural yogurt, to serve

1 Preheat the oven to 350°F. Grease and line the bottom of a 7-inch, square, shallow pan. Put the margarine, sugar, flour, egg, and milk in a bowl and beat until smooth.
2 Spoon the mixture into the pan and level the surface with the back of a spoon. Cook for 30 minutes or until well risen and set.
3 Meanwhile, warm the honey and lemon together. While it is still warm, prick the cake all over with a toothpick. Spoon over the honey mixture and leave until just warm. Cut in small squares or fingers. Crumble into a serving bowl and serve with yogurt.

Farina pudding

Fresh apricots or peaches make a nice contrast to the slightly gritty texture of farina. Chop them finely and stir them in prior to baking, or make a purée and stir it in just before serving.

1 Preheat the oven to 400°F. Grease a 2½ cup ovenproof dish. Finely chop the fruit and put it in a saucepan, with the milk and butter. Heat gently until the butter has melted.

2 Sprinkle in the farina, stirring continuously. Bring to a boil. Simmer for 3 minutes and then pour into the ovenproof dish. Cook for 30 minutes, or until the batter has set. Allow to cool slightly before serving.

MAKES: *4 portions*
PREPARATION TIME: *10 minutes*
COOKING TIME: *30 minutes*
FREEZING: *not recommended*

INGREDIENTS
2 fresh apricots or 1 peach, peeled and pitted
1¼ cups milk
1 tablespoon unsalted butter or margarine
3 tablespoons farina
1 teaspoon sugar

Pink coconut ice

A simple frozen dessert that doesn't take forever to prepare and can be enjoyed by everyone in the family.

1 Purée the raspberries in a blender or food processor until smooth. Strain to remove seeds. Whip the cream until soft peaks form. Stir in the coconut milk and fruit purée.

2 Pour the mixture into a rigid plastic box, cover and freeze for 2 hours. Using an electric mixer, beat the ice until smooth. Cover and freeze overnight, until solid.

MAKES: *1½ pints*
PREPARATION TIME: *15 minutes + freezing overnight*

INGREDIENTS
1 lb raspberries
1¼ cups whipping cream
14 oz can of coconut milk

HINTS AND TIPS
After the final beating, freeze portions in cleaned individual yogurt pots. Cover well. Remove the ice cream from the freezer 15 minutes before serving, to allow it to soften slightly.

Orange custard cream

This can be served warm or chilled according to your baby's preferences. A batch will keep for up to 1 month in the freezer.

MAKES: *2 portions*
PREPARATION TIME: *20 minutes*
COOKING TIME: *1 hour*
FREEZING: *recommended*

INGREDIENTS
1 1/4 cups milk
1/2 teaspoon vanilla extract
2 egg yolks
3 tablespoons sugar
grated peel of 1 orange

1 Preheat the oven to 400°F. Heat the milk until it is almost boiling. Meanwhile, mix together the vanilla, egg yolks, sugar, and orange peel. Whisk the milk into the orange mixture.
2 Pour into two small baking dishes or ovenproof cups. Put in a small roasting pan and fill the pan with boiling water to come halfway up the sides of the dishes.
3 Cook for 1 hour, or until just set. Serve with puréed or frozen orange segments.

Baked banana

If your baby enjoys bananas, one day you'll find a teenager in your kitchen making this recipe.

MAKES: *1 portion*
PREPARATION TIME: *5 minutes*
COOKING TIME: *10 minutes*
FREEZING: *not recommended*

INGREDIENTS
1 small banana, sliced
1 teaspoon unsalted butter
1/2 teaspoon lemon juice
1/4 teaspoon brown sugar
a pinch of ground cinnamon
sour cream, to serve

1 Preheat the oven to 350°F. Grease a 6-inch square of foil and place the banana in the center. Dot with butter then sprinkle the lemon juice, brown sugar, and cinnamon over it.
2 Wrap over and seal the foil parcel. Put in a baking dish and cook for 10 minutes, or until softened. Spoon into a serving dish and mash if necessary. Serve with a little sour cream.

SUPPER

Your inspiration and energy can be flagging toward the end of the day, so here is a variety of savories and a few sweet ideas for your baby to try. Many can be made in advance.

Cheese charlotte

A charlotte is a sweet or savory dish, baked in a mold. The cheesy custard in this version will make this a favorite.

1 Preheat the oven to 350°F. Grease four small baking pans or heatproof dishes. Using a 2½-inch cookie cutter, stamp out 12 rounds from the bread. Spread cream cheese over each round.
2 Put three cheesy rounds, cheese-side up, in each pan or dish. Beat the egg and milk together and then pour some over each pan or dish. Sprinkle Cheddar cheese on top.
3 Place the pans or dishes in a roasting pan and fill the pan with enough boiling water to come half way up the side of each dish. Cover with foil and bake for 30 minutes or until set. Cool slightly before serving.

MAKES: *4*
PREPARATION TIME: *25 minutes*
COOKING TIME: *30 minutes*
FREEZING: *recommended*

INGREDIENTS
6 thin slices of whole wheat bread
⅓ cup cream cheese
1 egg yolk
½ pint milk
¼ cup grated Cheddar cheese

Banana and date whip

This is suitable for tea, or for dessert after a light lunch. Try it with other fruit spreads.

Mash half the banana with the date spread until smooth. Stir in the custard. Chop the remaining banana finely and then stir it into the mashed-banana mixture.

MAKES: *1 portion*
PREPARATION TIME: *5 minutes*
FREEZING: *not recommended*

INGREDIENTS
1 small banana
1 teaspoon date spread
3 tablespoons vanilla custard or
  yogurt

MAKES: *4 portions*
PREPARATION TIME: *20 minutes*
FREEZING: *not recommended*

INGREDIENTS
1¼ cups milk
1 teaspoon cornstarch
3 tablespoons chopped fresh parsley
a pinch of ground nutmeg
2 oz cream cheese
*2 oz small animal-shaped or
    alphabet pasta*

Creamy herb pasta

**This makes quite a thin sauce to coat the pasta, but it will thicken
as it cools.**

1 Mix 3 tablespoons of milk with the cornstarch to form a smooth
paste. Heat the remaining milk almost to boiling and then stir in the
cornstarch.
2 Return to the saucepan and stir over a low heat until the
mixture bubbles and thickens. Stir in the parsley, nutmeg, and cream
cheese.
3 Meanwhile, cook the pasta in boiling water for 8 minutes or as
directed on the package. Drain and stir into the sauce. Chop or
blend briefly in a blender or food processor.

MAKES: *4 portions*
PREPARATION TIME: *10 minutes +
    15 minutes soaking*
COOKING TIME: *5 minutes*
FREEZING: *not recommended*

INGREDIENTS
2 oz cracked or bulghar wheat
1 oz raisins
⅔ cup hot vegetable stock
*1 strip each of red and green pepper,
    seeded and chopped*
1 oz corn
*1 firm ripe tomato, skinned,
    seeded and chopped*
FOR THE DRESSING:
2 teaspoons sunflower oil
1 teaspoon smooth peanut butter
½ teaspoon lemon juice

Cracked wheat salad

**Cracked wheat or bulghar wheat makes a great base for a baby's
first salad. If you prefer, use cooked brown rice.**

1 Soak the cracked wheat and raisins in the stock for 15 minutes.
2 Drain the stock into a saucepan through a heatproof strainer. Add
⅔ cup water to the retained stock and bring to a boil. Add the
peppers and corn.
3 Position the strainer containing the cracked wheat and raisins
over the pan, cover, and steam for 5 minutes, or until the vegetables
and cracked wheat are tender.
4 Meanwhile, mix the oil, peanut butter and lemon juice in a bowl.
5 Drain the vegetables and cracked wheat and stir them into the
dressing. Chop or blend briefly in a blender or food processor.

Chickadee puffs

Ready-prepared hummus, which is made from a purée of garbanzo beans and sesame seeds, adds protein to these tempting morsels, and the sesame-seed topping brings the flavor out. Try this with other root vegetables as well. The fresh tomato is a cooling and refreshing accompaniment, which also increases the level of vitamin C in the dish.

1 Cook the potato in boiling, salted water for 15 minutes, or until tender. Drain well and mash with the butter, milk, and hummus.
2 Preheat the oven to 400°F. Lightly grease a 12-hole muffin pan. Put a spoonful of potato mixture in each section and sprinkle with sesame seeds. Cook for 15 minutes, or until the top is golden. Serve with the chopped tomato.

MAKES: *12 puffs*
PREPARATION TIME: *15 minutes*
COOKING TIME: *30 minutes*
FREEZING: *not recommended*

INGREDIENTS
8 oz potato, peeled and chopped
1 tablespoon unsalted butter or margarine
1 tablespoon milk
1 tablespoon hummus
1/4 teaspoon sesame seeds
1 tomato, skinned, seeded and chopped

Buttons and bows

Tiny button mushrooms and bow-shaped pasta in a simple tomato sauce make a great supper for babies with hearty appetites.

1 Melt the butter in a saucepan and add the tomatoes, celery, and carrot. Simmer gently for 10 minutes.
2 Stir in the mushrooms and cook for a further 5 minutes, or until the vegetables are soft.
3 Meanwhile, cook the pasta in boiling water for 10 minutes, or until tender. Drain well. Stir into the mushroom mixture, with the mozzarella. Chop or blend briefly in blender or food processor.

MAKES: *4 portions*
PREPARATION TIME: *10 minutes*
COOKING TIME: *20 minutes*
FREEZING: *recommended*

INGREDIENTS
1 tablespoon unsalted butter or margarine
4 firm ripe tomatoes, skinned, seeded and chopped
1 oz celery, washed and finely chopped
1 oz carrot, finely chopped
1 1/2 oz button mushrooms, wiped and chopped
2 oz bow-shaped pasta
1 oz mozzarella cheese, cut in tiny pieces

MAKES: *4 portions*
PREPARATION AND COOKING TIME:
   35 minutes
FREEZING: *recommended*

INGREDIENTS
1 ¹/₄ cups milk
1 bay leaf
4 oz macaroni or small pasta shapes
1 oz unsalted butter or margarine
4 tablespoons flour
¹/₂ cup grated Gruyère cheese

Mini-macaroni cheese

My son virtually lived on this when he was 7 months old. It is high in calcium, and I account for his good teeth by his early preference for this recipe.

1 Heat the milk with the bay leaf until almost boiling. Remove from the heat, cover and leave to infuse.
2 Cook the macaroni in boiling water for 10 minutes, or as directed on the package, until tender. Drain well.
3 Melt the butter in a clean pan, remove from the heat and stir in the flour. Remove the bay leaf from the milk and discard it. Gradually stir the milk into the pan.
4 Stir the sauce over a medium heat until thickened. Simmer for 3 minutes and then stir in half the cheese and all the macaroni. Spoon into four small baking pans or heatproof dishes. Preheat the broiler.
5 Sprinkle the remaining cheese over each and cook under the broiler until golden.

MAKES: *1 portion*
PREPARATION TIME: *5 minutes*
FREEZING: *not recommended*

INGREDIENTS
half a ripe avocado
¹/₂ teaspoon lemon juice
¹/₄ cup cottage cheese
¹/₂ teaspoon date spread

Avocado cream

Avocados are little orbs of pure energy and packed with vitamins. They mash superbly and go well with a variety of other flavors. Lemon juice prevents the avocado from discoloring.

1 Using a teaspoon, scoop out the avocado flesh from the skin and mash it with the lemon juice, cottage cheese, and date spread.
2 Spoon back into the skin or spoon into the feeding bowl.

HINTS AND TIPS
As a baby will only manage half of an avocado at a sitting, retain the pit in the uneaten piece, sprinkle with lemon juice, and wrap in plastic wrap. Keep chilled and eat within 24 hours.

Creamed mushrooms

The egg-yellow oyster or chanterelle mushrooms cook to a lovely, creamy texture and make a tasty change from the cultivated varieties in this version of a traditional favorite. If you can't get them, though, any kind of mushroom can be used; the flavor is better if you can use more than one variety.

1 Cook the mushrooms and onion in melted butter for 5 minutes, or until softened. Mix together the cornstarch and milk and stir them into the pan.
2 Stir over low heat until the sauce thickens. Crumble in the rice cake and stir well. Leave for a few minutes before serving to allow the rice cake to soften somewhat.

MAKES: *1 portion*
PREPARATION TIME: *5 minutes*
COOKING TIME: *5 minutes*
FREEZING: *not recommended*

INGREDIENTS
1 oz mushrooms, chopped
1 green onion, white part only,
  finely chopped
1 tablespoon unsalted butter or
  margarine
1 teaspoon cornstarch
1/2 cup milk
1/2 unsalted rice cake

Applejack afternooner

Good old-fashioned apple sauce comes into its own again, because it is so versatile and nutritious.

1 Cook the flaked rice or instant rice in simmering milk for 10 minutes, stirring occasionally, until thickened. Stir in the apple sauce, ground almonds and almond extract.
2 Cool a little before serving.

MAKES: *1 portion*
PREPARATION TIME: *3 minutes*
COOKING TIME: *10 minutes*
FREEZING: *not recommended*

INGREDIENTS
1 tablespoon flaked rice or instant
  rice
2/3 cup milk
1/4 cup apple purée
1 teaspoon ground almonds
1/2 drop almond extract

> **HINTS AND TIPS**
> *For older babies, substitute raw grated apple for the apple sauce.*

Cottage bake

It's not worth putting your oven on to cook just one potato, but this is a good dish to make when the oven is on for baking.

MAKES: *1 portion*
PREPARATION TIME: *10 minutes*
COOKING TIME: *1 hour*
FREEZING: *not recommended*

INGREDIENTS
6 oz potato, scrubbed
1 tablespoon cottage cheese
1 oz carrot, grated
1 oz zucchini, grated

1 Preheat the oven to 400°F. Prick the potato and bake it in the oven for 1 hour, or until tender. Halve and scoop out the flesh with a teaspoon.
2 Mash together the potato, cottage cheese, carrot. and zucchini. Spoon back into potato skin or feeding bowl.

Cowboy beans

Some babies may find this a little indigestible, so feed it to babies over 9 months.

MAKES: *1 portion*
PREPARATION TIME: *5 minutes*
COOKING TIME: *3 minutes*
FREEZING: *not recommended*

INGREDIENTS
3 tablespoons baked beans in tomato sauce
1 tablespoon cooked or canned red kidney beans
1/2 teaspoon Worcestershire sauce
1 thin slice of whole wheat bread
1 teaspoon softened unsalted butter or margarine
yeast extract, for spreading

1 Heat all the beans and Worcestershire sauce. Mash or blend them briefly in a blender or food processor.
2 Meanwhile, toast the bread. Using a star-shaped cookie cutter, stamp out shapes and spread with butter and a very thin coating of yeast extract.

HINTS AND TIPS
Try spreading toast with a thin layer of smooth peanut butter as an alternative to yeast extract.

Melon cooler

A refreshing dish for a hot day or to soothe teething gums. Choose a fairly firm-textured melon for this, such as a canteloupe or honeydew, as opposed to the more watery types, or the melon ice will not have such a good texture.

1 Line a square, shallow dish with plastic wrap. Blend the melon, milk, and coconut in a blender or food processor until smooth. Pour into the dish, cover and freeze overnight.
2 Put the melon ice in a bowl and crush it with a masher. Serve with extra chopped melon or fruit purée.

MAKES: *1 portion*
PREPARATION TIME: *8 minutes + freezing overnight*
FREEZING: *not recommended*

INGREDIENTS
⅛th of a melon, skinned and seeded
⅔ cup milk
1 tablespoon flaked coconut
extra melon, chopped, or fruit purée, to serve

Potato patacakes

Make these in the morning, or when you have some mashed potato left over. Once made, they cook quickly.

1 Cook the potato in boiling water for 15 minutes. Add the mixed vegetables and return to a boil. Simmer for 5 minutes or until the vegetables are tender. Drain well.
2 Mash the vegetables with butter and milk until fairly smooth. Using dampened hands, divide the mixture into six portions and shape into rounds.
3 Mix the bread crumbs and ground almonds together and use to coat each patacake. Chill until required.
4 Heat the oil in a large, non-stick frying pan. Fry the patacakes for 4–5 minutes each side, until golden. Drain on paper towels. Cool for a few minutes before serving. Serve with a little tomato catsup or homemade tomato paste.

MAKES: *6 patacakes*
PREPARATION TIME: *15 minutes*
COOKING TIME: *30 minutes*
FREEZING: *not recommended*

INGREDIENTS
8 oz potato, peeled and chopped
3 oz frozen chopped mixed vegetables, e.g., peas, corn, peppers, green beans, celery
1 tablespoon unsalted butter or margarine
1 tablespoon milk
⅓ cup fresh whole wheat bread crumbs
⅓ cup ground almonds
2 teaspoons oil

Toddlers
and children

18 MONTHS ONWARD

*B*y the time your toddler reaches the second birthday, you will probably have established some form of eating routine and mealtimes can be more relaxed occasions. You no longer have the bother of sterilizing, and your little one will have become quite adept at feeding him- or herself.

Making mealtimes fun

At 18 months, you may like to buy your child its own cutlery set. This encourages more independence, and makes mealtimes fun. It may be tricky to teach the correct way to hold the cutlery at first: toddlers tend to be ambidextrous, so don't be too worried if your child uses the fork and spoon in the same way as the shovel from the sandpit. If you are really keen to encourage proper use of cutlery, look out for the children's cutlery that has raised bumps on the handles, to show where fingers and thumbs should be placed.

You will probably begin to encourage your child to have good table manners without setting out to do so. From the time the child is in the high chair, the phrases "please" and "thank you," or at least "thanks," will have been reinforced and so it is only natural that you extend these to the dining table. You will have your own opinion about the importance of formal table manners; the leading-by-example method is usually effective in setting the standards you want. It is not too much to expect that children should be able to say please and thank you by the age of three, before they begin nursery or playgroup; by school age they should be able to leave cutlery in the correct position on the plate at the end of a meal and ask to be excused from the table.

Encourage good table manners by allowing your child to feed him or herself with their own dinner set. For toddlers, a plate with a weighted base helps reduce risk of spills.

Invitations to dine

Nursery school, play group and joining other children for lunch or at birthday parties will help your child put these lessons into practice. This will also help him or her to exert independence. As a vegetarian, you may be concerned that your child will be tempted to try the hot dogs, hamburgers, and chicken nuggets that are often available at these gatherings. To overcome this, let the nursery school or play group know of your preferences for your child's food. If no provision is made for a vegetarian meal (and nowadays there often is) it is a good idea to pack a lunch for your child to take. Brightly colored lunch boxes are available from most major stores, and will make the owner feel very grown up. Mysteriously, food always seems to disappear from a lunch box, so if your child is a fussy eater, you may like to try packing a lunch box even for eating at home. Tea or birthday parties may be a little more awkward, as you do not wish to offend the hosts or make your child stand out. Honesty is the best policy: simply tell the parents that your child is vegetarian and keep your fingers crossed that they steer the meat dishes away. Anyway, even the youngest of vegetarians, offered a choice, tends to stick to the foods that are familiar.

Pack them off to school with their own plastic easy-clean lunch box! Many children prefer to eat a home-packed lunch and you will be able to control what they are eating away from home.

Menu planner
Your four-week toddler mealtime guide

	Breakfast	**Lunch**	**Snack**
Week 1			
Day 1	Bran Tub	Eggplant and Lentil Bolognese; fruit fromage frais	Moonbeams
Day 2	Corn Muffins	Stir-fry with Egg Wheels; Rice and Golden Raisin Pudding	Mexican Beans; banana
Day 3	Swiss-style Muesli	Tomato and Spinach Pie; Toffee Creams	Muffin Clock; canned mandarin oranges and yogurt
Day 4	Alimoes	Barley Pilaf; Easy Apple Pie	Spotty Dogs; Date Bars
Day 5	Speckled Egg-scramble	Rice Baskets; Surprise Mice	Tic-Tac-Toe; fruit yogurt
Day 6	Honeydew Refresher	Sloppy Joes; Toffee Creams and apple wedges	Sandwich Snails
Day 7	Mushroom Kedgeree	Vegetable Crunchies; Teeny Trifles	Cheesy Toast Squares; fruit fromage frais
Week 2			
Day 1	Swiss-style Muesli	Vegetable Lasagne; Surprise Mice	Smiley Clown; Frosted Carrot Cake
Day 2	Toast and Dried-Fruit spread	Southern-style Rice and Beans; Bread and Butter Pudding	Scorched Corn; fruit yogurt
Day 3	Shredded Wheat and sliced banana	Peanut Powerballs; Easy Apple Pie	Tomato Piperade; Fun Fingers
Day 4	Waffles with Apple Syrup	Mixed Bean and Spinach Pot; Knights, Castles and Custard	Quick Cannelloni; canned peach and yogurt
Day 5	Bran Tub	Spring Rolls; Fried Rice; Teeny Trifle	Spotty Dogs; Fun Fingers
Day 6	Lemon Griddle Cakes	Creamy Corn Pasta Spirals; Toffee Cream	Tic-Tac-Toe; fresh pear
Day 7	Mushroom Kedgeree	Lightning Burgers; Home-baked Beans; Surprise Mice	Double Deckers; ice cream
Week 3 Same as week 1			
Week 4 Same as week 2			

Remember, these menus are just suggestions to help you provide your child with a nutritionally balanced and varied diet. Always provide toddlers with a drink at mealtimes; this is best given after the meal, otherwise, water or juice will fill them up too quickly. Relax this rule during hot weather, and particularly if there's been some strenuous playing. Drinks before bedtime is rather a contentious issue. It shouldn't matter if you have a toddler still in diapers. If you are trying to get your child to stay dry during the night, a drink about an hour before bed is the best idea.

BREAKFASTS

Small children probably have their last meal at four or five o'clock, and they may then not eat until seven o'clock the next morning, a gap of 14 hours or more, so breakfast is vital. By the time they reach the toddler stage, many children will already have their favorite foods. But you need to balance the week's breakfast menus, to make sure they are getting all the nutrition and energy they need. Serve high-protein, energy-boosting foods, combining fruit with yogurt, bread, or cereals.

MAKES: *16 griddle cakes*
PREPARATION TIME: *10 minutes*
COOKING TIME: *25 minutes*
FREEZING: *recommended*

INGREDIENTS
FOR THE STRAWBERRY SAUCE:
12 oz fresh strawberries, hulled and chopped
1 tablespoon superfine sugar
juice of 1/2 an orange
FOR THE GRIDDLE CAKES:
1/2 cup self-rising unbleached white flour
good 1/2 cup self-rising whole wheat flour
1 large egg
2/3 cup milk
grated peel of 1 unwaxed lemon
1 teaspoon corn oil

Lemon griddle cakes

To save time, prepare the batter the night before and chill it until needed. The fruit sauce boosts the body with vitamins A and C and the griddle cakes, though low in fat, provide energy and fiber.

1 Cook the strawberries in a small saucepan, with the sugar and orange juice, for 5 minutes, or until soft. Allow to cool.
2 Sift the flour together, adding the bran left in the sifter to the bowl at the end. Beat the egg and milk together. Make a well in the center of the flour and stir in the egg mixture and the lemon peel. Beat well until smooth.
3 Heat a non-stick griddle, or a large frying pan. Add the corn oil, and then wipe away any excess with a paper towel. Spoon about 5 tablespoonfuls of the batter on to the griddle, allowing room for spreading. Cook for 2–3 minutes over medium heat, until the surface begins to bubble. Flip the griddle cake over and cook the second side until it is golden.
4 Keep the griddle cake warm in a clean dish towel while you cook the remainder. Serve with the strawberry sauce.

Corn muffins

A fun alternative to toast, these individual muffins take no time at all to bake and taste delicious. To save time for another day, make a double batch and freeze what's left. Serve the muffins spread with butter or margarine, and fruit spread.

1 Preheat the oven to 400°F. Lightly grease a six-cup muffin pan with oil. Sift the flour, cornmeal and baking powder together into a mixing bowl, adding the bran left in the sifter to the bowl at the end.
2 Beat together the egg, honey, and milk. Make a well in the center of the dry ingredients and add the egg mixture. Gently stir until the mixture just comes together; do not over-beat it, or you will knock out the air and the muffins will not rise.
3 Divide the mixture between the six cups in the prepared pan and bake the muffins for 12–15 minutes, or until they are well risen and golden.

MAKES: *6 muffins*
PREPARATION TIME: *10 minutes*
COOKING TIME: *15 minutes*
FREEZING: *recommended*

INGREDIENTS
¾ cup whole wheat flour
½ cup cornmeal
1½ teaspoons baking powder
1 large egg, beaten
1 tablespoon clear honey
⅔ cup milk

MAKES: *4 waffles*
PREPARATION TIME: *10 minutes*
COOKING TIME: *8 minutes*
FREEZING: *not recommended*

INGREDIENTS

1/3 cup unsweetened apple juice
3 tablespoons clear honey
1 tablespoon light soft brown sugar
6 tablespoons unbleached self-rising white flour
3 tablespoons self-rising whole wheat flour
1 teaspoon superfine sugar
1 large egg, separated
1 tablespoon corn oil
2/3 cup milk

Waffles with apple syrup

Children love to see these made and are delighted when the waffle magically appears from the iron. The waffles are full of protein, as well as calcium to aid bone development. One point, though: serve the accompanying syrup sparingly, as it is high in sugar.

1 Heat the apple juice, honey and brown sugar in a saucepan until dissolved. Bring to a boil and boil for 2–3 minutes, or until syrupy. Allow to cool.
2 Sift the flours together, adding the bran left in the sifter at the end to the bowl. Stir in the sugar. Make a well in the center and add the egg yolk and oil. Gradually beat in the milk to form a smooth batter.
3 Lightly grease the waffle iron with oil. Heat the waffle iron as directed by the manufacturer. Meanwhile, whisk the egg white until soft peaks form. Fold the egg white into the waffle batter.
4 Pour the batter into the waffle iron, close the iron and cook for 2–3 minutes. Turn over (if not using an electric model) and cook the second side until the waffle is golden and can be removed easily. Keep warm while cooking the rest of the batter. Serve the waffles with a little of the apple syrup.

MAKES: *about 1 lb*
PREPARATION TIME: *5 minutes*
COOKING TIME: *20 minutes*
FREEZING: *not recommended*

INGREDIENTS

3 oz dried peaches, finely chopped
6 oz dried pitted dates, finely chopped
6 oz ready-to-eat dried apricots, finely chopped
grated peel of 1/2 unwaxed lemon and 1/2 unwaxed orange
a pinch of ground cinnamon
2/3 cup apple or orange juice

Dried-fruit spread

Dried fruit is a concentrated source of iron, calcium and potassium. Use this easy-to-make spread in place of high-sugar jam. It will keep for up to two weeks in a covered container, if you store it in the refrigerator.

1 Boil a 16 oz preserving jar for 3 minutes. Remove from the pan with tongs and set the jar to dry in a warm oven while you prepare the spread.
2 Put all the ingredients in a saucepan and bring them to a boil. Reduce the heat and simmer very gently for 20 minutes, stirring occasionally, until the mixture has thickened and the fruit juice has evaporated. Add extra apple or orange juice if the mixture sticks during cooking.
3 Mash the mixture until smooth and then spoon it into the prepared jar. Seal, label and cool according to your preserving instructions.

Speckled egg-scramble

My son calls these "eggs with grass" but he enjoys the flavor and bright-green color that the fresh herbs add to humdrum scrambled eggs. Remember to cook the eggs until firm for youngsters, because of the danger of salmonella poisoning, and don't give this to children under three years old. Serve with toast, corn muffins, or waffles.

Melt the butter in a saucepan. Beat the egg and milk together and then stir them into the butter. Sprinkle in the herbs and stir over low heat until the mixture thickens.

SERVES: *1*
PREPARATION TIME: *5 minutes*
COOKING TIME: *5 minutes*
FREEZING: *not recommended*

INGREDIENTS
1 teaspoon butter or margarine
1 large egg
1/3 cup milk
2 teaspoons chopped fresh herbs, e.g. parsley, chives or chervil

Mushroom kedgeree

This can be served for breakfast as well as for dinner. It tastes best with brown rice, which is far more nutritious than white but needs a little extra cooking time.

1 Heat the oil in a saucepan and add the mushrooms and green onion. Cook over medium heat for 5 minutes. Stir in the rice and cook for 3–4 minutes, or until the rice is shiny. Add the stock and the turmeric and bring to a boil. Cover and simmer for 30 minutes, or until tender.
2 Shell the hard boiled egg and cut it in wedges. Slice the tomato. Serve the kedgeree with the pieces of egg and tomato.

SERVES: *2*
PREPARATION TIME: *15 minutes*
COOKING TIME: *35 minutes*
FREEZING: *not recommended*

INGREDIENTS
2 teaspoons vegetable oil
2 oz button mushrooms, wiped and sliced
1 green onion, white only, finely chopped
1/4 cup long-grain brown rice
1 1/4 cups vegetable stock
a pinch of ground turmeric
1 hard boiled egg
1 tomato

SERVES: *4*
PREPARATION TIME: *15 minutes*
FREEZING: *not recommended*

INGREDIENTS
1 honeydew melon
2 blood oranges
4 oz seedless grapes, washed and dried
1/2 cup sparkling apple juice

Honeydew refresher

A light mixture of melon, oranges and grapes that you can serve on its own with yogurt or make more substantial with cereal. It's high in vitamin C and natural sugar for energy and you can store it for up to two days in the refrigerator.

1 Halve the melon and scoop out the seeds. Cut the flesh in wedges, remove the skin and slice the flesh into a child's bite-size pieces. Put the pieces in a serving bowl.
2 Using a very sharp knife, peel oranges, holding the fruit over the bowl, and then carefully remove each segment. Halve the segments and add them to the bowl, with the grapes. Stir in the apple juice just before serving.

SERVES: *1*
PREPARATION TIME: *5 minutes*
FREEZING: *not recommended*

INGREDIENTS
3 tablespoons muesli
1/3 cup natural yogurt
1/3 cup half-and-half or cream

Swiss-style muesli

This has to be made the night before, so it is great for a frantic morning, when time is short. The oats and fruit in the muesli soften during soaking, resulting in a delicious, thick, creamy porridge, which the whole family will enjoy.

Spoon the muesli into a serving bowl and then stir in the yogurt and half-and-half or cream. Cover and chill overnight. Stir before serving.

HINTS AND TIPS
Use home-made muesli or an unsweetened commercial kind, but avoid those varieties that contain nuts, which will become unpleasantly soggy. Substitute fruit juice if your child cannot tolerate dairy products.

Alimoes

A breakfast based on sautéed potatoes with mushrooms and tomatoes, which my father used to make for me as a child. Use potatoes that have been cooked in their skins, for extra fiber and vitamin C.

1 Heat the oil in a non-stick frying pan. Add the potato and cook over medium heat for 10 minutes, or until golden. Drain on paper towels and keep hot.

2 Add the mushrooms to the pan and cook for 5 minutes. Add the tomato wedges and cook for 3–4 minutes more, or until the mushrooms are tender and the tomatoes heated through.

3 Spoon the potato into a serving bowl and top with mushroom mixture. Sprinkle with the chives.

SERVES: *2*
PREPARATION TIME: *10 minutes*
COOKING TIME: *20 minutes*
FREEZING: *not recommended*

INGREDIENTS
1 tablespoon corn oil
6 oz cooked potato, cut in large chunks
2 oz mushrooms, wiped and sliced
1 large tomato, cored and cut in wedges
1 teaspoon snipped fresh chives

Bran tub

Add a surprise to breakfast time by putting a slice of fruit, a whole strawberry or a cherry in the bottom of your child's cereal dish. Children will eat quickly to reach the treat at the bottom in no time; it's a good way to encourage a "picky" eater.

Place the fruit in the bottom of a clear tumbler or sundae dish. Layer the yogurt and the bran and oatmeal mixture in the dish, ending with a dollop of yogurt. Sprinkle with the turbinado sugar before serving.

SERVES: *1*
PREPARATION TIME: *5 minutes*
FREEZING: *not recommended*

INGREDIENTS
1 whole strawberry, pitted cherry, mandarin orange segment or a slice of your child's favorite fruit
2/3 cup yogurt
1 tablespoon bran
1 tablespoon oatmeal, toasted
a pinch of turbinado or raw sugar

HINTS AND TIPS
Any breakfast cereal can be used with yogurt in this dish. Some children may prefer fruit yogurt.

LUNCHES

Often lunch is a child's main meal, so it must be substantial enough to provide at least a third of the daily nutritional requirements. All the recipes in this chapter have been designed with this requirement in mind. Tasty main-meal ideas, packed with the goodness of pulses, grains and vegetables, will satisfy the fussiest eaters.

SERVES: *1*
PREPARATION TIME: *5 minutes*
COOKING TIME: *10 minutes*
FREEZING: *not recommended*

INGREDIENTS

1 teaspoon butter or margarine
1 small leek, trimmed, washed and finely sliced
2 oz baby corn, washed and chopped
2 oz frozen peas
1 oz canned red kidney beans, rinsed
1 teaspoon cornstarch
²/3 cup milk
1 oz three-colored (tricolore) pasta spirals
1/2 oz carrot, grated

Creamy corn pasta spirals

A versatile sauce that can be spooned over baked potatoes as well as served with pasta, as described here. The grated carrot topping adds vitamins A and C.

1 Melt the butter or margarine in a saucepan and cook the leek and corn for 5 minutes, or until tender. Stir in the peas and beans and cook for 2–3 minutes.
2 Mix the cornstarch and milk together until smooth and then stir the mixture into the pan. Stir over medium heat until the sauce thickens and is smooth. Simmer gently for a few minutes.
3 Meanwhile, cook the pasta in boiling water for 10 minutes, or as directed on the package. Drain well. Spoon the pasta into a serving bowl and pour over the sauce. Sprinkle the grated carrot on top before serving.

Vegetable lasagne

Children love pasta, but they often give vegetables the thumbs-down. If this is your problem, try disguising vegetables in this tasty package under a blanket of cheesy sauce.

1 Heat the oil in a saucepan and fry the onion for 5 minutes, or until softened. Add the remaining vegetables and cook for 5 minutes more. Stir in the tomatoes, tomato catsup and stock. Bring the liquid to a boil and leave to simmer for 20 minutes. Preheat the oven to 350°F.

2 Meanwhile, to make the sauce, melt the butter or margarine in a clean pan. Add the flour and cook for 1 minute. Remove the pan from the heat and gradually stir in the milk. Stir over medium heat until the sauce thickens and comes to a boil. Add half the cheese to the sauce and season with nutmeg.

3 Spoon half the vegetable mixture into the base of a 2½ cup ovenproof dish. Top with a sheet of lasagne.

4 Spoon half the cheese sauce on top of the lasagne and then spoon on the remaining vegetable mixture. Place the second sheet of lasagne on top and then spoon over the remaining cheese sauce to cover the lasagne completely.

5 Sprinkle with the remaining cheese and cook in the oven for 35–40 minutes, or until the lasagne is tender and the top golden. Allow to cool slightly and then serve, with wedges of baby lettuce and tomato.

SERVES: *2*
PREPARATION TIME: *20 minutes*
COOKING TIME: *1 hour 10 minutes*
FREEZING: *recommended*

INGREDIENTS
2 teaspoons sunflower oil
¼ onion, finely chopped
3 oz zucchini, cut in tiny cubes
3 oz carrot, cut in tiny cubes
2 oz button mushrooms, wiped and
  quartered
1 strip each, red and green pepper,
  seeded and chopped
1 oz frozen corn
⅓ cup canned chopped tomatoes
  with herbs
2 teaspoons tomato catsup
⅔ cup vegetable stock
FOR THE CHEESE SAUCE:
2 tablespoons butter or margarine
4 tablespoons unbleached all-purpose
  flour
1¼ cups milk
⅓ cup grated Cheddar or Colby
  cheese
a pinch of grated nutmeg
2 sheets of no-cook lasagne

HINTS AND TIPS
If you like, make this in two smaller containers and freeze the second portion.

Southern-style rice and beans

A hearty winter dish inspired by the rich bean stews of the southern United States. Children can easily eat this without help, because the rice sticks the other ingredients together as they are gathered on the spoon. Serve with carrot sticks.

SERVES: *2*
PREPARATION TIME: *15 minutes*
COOKING TIME: *35 minutes*
FREEZING: *not recommended*

INGREDIENTS
2 teaspoons corn oil
¼ onion, finely chopped
1 small garlic clove, crushed
1 strip each red and green pepper, seeded and chopped
2 oz mushrooms, wiped and chopped
¼ cup long-grain white rice
⅓ cup chopped canned tomatoes
1¼ cups vegetable stock
a pinch of dried marjoram
½ teaspoon corn or maple syrup
2 oz green cabbage, shredded
1 oz small frozen peas
1 oz cooked red kidney beans

1 Heat the oil in a saucepan and cook the onion and garlic for 5 minutes, or until softened. Stir in the peppers and mushrooms. Cook for 5 minutes. Add the rice, tomatoes, stock and marjoram. Bring to a boil.
2 Stir in the corn or maple syrup, cover and simmer for 15 minutes.
3 Add the cabbage, peas and kidney beans and return to boiling. Cook for 10 minutes, stirring occasionally.

Stir-fry with egg wheels

The egg wheels provide protein and calcium in this colorful stir-fry and they are no more difficult to make than an omelet. Serve with egg noodles, if your child likes them. Children enjoy the novelty of using grown-up china or cutlery, so if you have them, serve this in little Chinese bowls with Chinese-style spoons.

1 Beat the egg with the soy sauce. Heat half the oil in a 7-inch non-stick omelet pan. Add the egg and cook over medium heat for 3 minutes, or until set. Flip the omelet over and cook the second side until golden.

2 Turn out the omelet on to a flat plate. When it's cool enough to handle, roll it up tightly and reserve it for later.

3 Heat the remaining oil in the frying-pan and stir fry all the vegetables, except the bean sprouts and pea pods, for 4–5 minutes. Add the bean sprouts, pea pods and the stir-fry sauce and cook for 3 minutes.

3 Spoon the vegetables into a serving bowl. Slice the omelet into ½-inch wheels and arrange on top.

SERVES: *1*
PREPARATION TIME: *15 minutes*
COOKING TIME: *10 minutes*
FREEZING: *not recommended*

INGREDIENTS
1 large egg
1 tablespoon low-sodium soy sauce
2 teaspoons peanut oil
2 oz carrot
2 oz zucchini
1 strip each yellow and red pepper, seeded and cut in matchsticks
1 oz fresh bean sprouts, washed
1 oz snow-pea pods, trimmed and sliced
1 teaspoon sweet and sour stir-fry sauce

Barley pilaf

A pilaf is a Middle Eastern dish consisting of lightly spiced vegetables with rice. It's usually made just with rice, but adding barley, which is rich in vitamins and minerals, adds interest and nutrition. Serve with cucumber and celery sticks.

1 Heat the oil in a saucepan and cook the onion over medium heat until softened. Stir in the spices, rice and barley and cook until shiny.

2 Stir in the stock, carrot and zucchini and bring to a boil. Reduce the heat, cover and simmer for 25 minutes.

3 Add the raisins and garbanzo beans. Cook for 5 minutes, or until heated through.

SERVES: *2*
PREPARATION TIME: *15 minutes*
COOKING TIME: *35 minutes*
FREEZING: *not recommended*

INGREDIENTS
1 teaspoon olive oil
¼ small onion, finely chopped
¼ teaspoon each ground cinnamon and ground coriander
1 oz long-grain brown rice
1½ oz pearl barley
2 cups vegetable stock
½ carrot, peeled and cut in sticks
½ zucchini, cubed
1 oz golden raisins
1 oz cooked garbanzo beans

INGREDIENTS

2 teaspoons olive oil

*2 oz each cooked red kidney beans,
    lima beans, garbanzo beans*

1 green onion, trimmed and chopped

1 garlic clove, crushed

2 tomatoes, skinned and chopped

1 teaspoon tomato catsup

1 oz young spinach leaves, washed

8 oz potato, peeled and chopped

3 tablespoons milk

Mixed bean and spinach pot

*A protein-rich main course that is also full of iron and potassium
(which is necessary to balance and correct the body's water
content). Smaller children may prefer the filling to be mashed.
Serve with green beans.*

1 Heat the oil in a saucepan and cook all the beans, the green onion
and the garlic over medium heat for 4–5 minutes. Stir in the tomatoes and catsup and cook for 5 minutes more.

2 Meanwhile, put the spinach leaves into a clean pan and cook over
low heat, stirring frequently, until wilted. Remove the spinach, add
the potatoes to the pan and cover them with cold water. Bring the
water to a boil, reduce the heat and simmer for 15 minutes, or until
tender. Drain the potatoes and mash them with the spinach and
milk. Preheat the broiler to hot.

3 Divide the bean mixture between two 1 cup heatproof dishes.
Spoon the mashed potato and spinach mixture on top and cook
under the broiler until the topping is golden.

HINTS AND TIPS

*For a richer version, stir some grated
cheese into the topping and sprinkle
over some more before broiling.*

Sloppy joes

Vegetarian ground meat is available ready-seasoned, so check you use the low-sodium (unseasoned) variety for children.

1 Preheat the oven to 400°F. Put the potatoes in a shallow dish and drizzle over 1 teaspoon oil. Cook the potatoes in the oven for 1 hour, or until they are golden. Turn the potatoes in the oil from time to time so they brown evenly all over.
2 Heat the remaining oil in a saucepan and cook the onion for 5 minutes, or until softened. Stir in remaining ingredients and bring to a boil. Simmer, stirring occasionally for 20 minutes, or until thickened and tender.
3 Arrange the potato wedges in a star pattern on a serving plate and spoon the vegetarian mixture into the center. Allow to cool slightly before serving.

SERVES: *1*
PREPARATION TIME: *15 minutes*
COOKING TIME: *1 hour*
FREEZING: *recommended*

INGREDIENTS
6 oz potato, scrubbed and cut in wedges
2 teaspoons corn oil
1/4 onion, finely chopped
2 oz carrot, grated
2 oz parsnip, grated
1/2 cup canned tomatoes
2 oz vegetarian ground meat
1 oz frozen peas
1 teaspoon barbecue sauce

Eggplant and lentil Bolognese

Vegetarian Bolognese sauces are among the best of vegetarian versions of classic dishes. Adults will enjoy this too.

1 Heat the oil in a saucepan and add the green onion, eggplant, carrot and peppers. Cook over a medium heat for 10 minutes, or until softened. Stir in the lentils, tomatoes, stock and tomato catsup. Bring to a boil. Sprinkle in the oregano, cover the pan and simmer for 20 minutes, or until the mixture has thickened slightly and the vegetables and lentils are tender.
2 Meanwhile, cook the pasta in a pan of boiling water for 10 minutes, or as directed on the package. Drain well. If you are using spaghetti, break it up. Spoon the pasta into a serving dish and top it with the vegetable and lentil mixture. Sprinkle over the cheese just before serving.

SERVES: *2*
PREPARATION TIME: *20 minutes*
COOKING TIME: *30 minutes*
FREEZING: *not recommended*

INGREDIENTS
2 teaspoons sunflower oil
1 green onion, trimmed and finely chopped
2 oz eggplant, cubed finely
3 oz carrot, cubed finely
1 strip each red and green pepper, seeded and chopped
3 tablespoons red lentils
1/3 cup canned chopped tomatoes
1/2 cup vegetable stock
2 teaspoons tomato catsup
a pinch of dried oregano
2 oz spaghetti or pasta shapes
1/4 cup grated Cheddar cheese

SNACK LUNCHES

The recipes in this section are lighter than the main meals in the previous section, and many can be prepared in advance so you can produce something quickly when your child needs "topping up." If your child can't eat all they need from a main meal at one sitting, these recipes will be invaluable.

SERVES: *2*
PREPARATION TIME: *15 minutes*
COOKING TIME: *20 minutes*
FREEZING: *recommended*

INGREDIENTS
1 small red pepper, halved lengthwise and seeded
1 teaspoon sunflower oil
2 oz button mushrooms, wiped and sliced
3 tablespoons long-grain white rice
1 teaspoon smooth peanut butter
1 cup vegetable stock
2 oz small broccoli flowerets
2 oz cooked red kidney beans
1 oz fresh or frozen corn

Rice baskets

Colorful little baskets of rice and vegetables, these are overflowing with goodness. Your child may need help to cut up the pepper basket, once the filling has been eaten. Serve with a sesame breadstick.

1 Blanch the pepper halves in boiling water for 4 minutes, or until just tender. Drain well.
2 Heat the oil in a saucepan, add the mushrooms and cook for 3 minutes. Stir in the rice and peanut butter and cook over medium heat for 1 minute. Pour over the stock and bring to a boil. Cover and simmer for 5 minutes.
3 Add the broccoli, kidney beans and corn and cook for 5 minutes more, or until the rice is tender. Spoon the mixture equally between the pepper halves.

HINTS AND TIPS
The peppers will become soggy if frozen, so it's best to freeze the filling only.

Lightning burgers

So called because, once made, they disappear in a flash. Keep a batch handy, individually wrapped, in the freezer. They cook perfectly well without being thawed first. Serve in a toasted sesame bun, with frilly lettuce, sliced tomatoes, and relish. Cut in halves or quarters before serving to small children.

1 Mix together the vegetarian ground meat, onion, carrot, and bread crumbs. Stir in the stock. Allow to cool slightly and then add the egg and yeast extract. Allow to cool completely.
2 Using moistened hands, shape the mixture into six burgers, using a 3-inch plain pastry cutter as a guide. Put the burgers on a baking sheet and chill until required.
3 Cook under a preheated broiler or lightly fry for 10 minutes, turning once, until cooked through.

MAKES: *6 burgers*
PREPARATION TIME: *30 minutes*
COOKING TIME: *20 minutes*
FREEZING: *recommended, after step 2*

INGREDIENTS
12 oz vegetarian ground meat
1 small onion, grated
1 small carrot, grated
2 cups fresh whole wheat bread crumbs
1 1/4 cups hot vegetable stock
1 large egg
1/4 teaspoon yeast extract

Vegetable crunchies

Smooth peanut butter adds protein and helps to bind the ingredients together in these tasty fingers. Serve with spaghetti hoops in tomato sauce.

1 Cook the potatoes in boiling water for 10 minutes. Add the mixed vegetables and green onion and cook for 5 minutes. Drain well.
2 Remove the potatoes and mash them with the peanut butter and milk, until smooth. Stir in the vegetables and allow to cool completely.
3 Beat the egg. On a plate, mix together the bread crumbs, cheese and sesame seeds. Divide the vegetable mixture into eight equal portions. Shape into small finger-length rectangles.
4 Coat each finger in egg and then in the crumb mixture. Chill until needed.
5 Heat about 1 tablespoon of oil in a non-stick frying pan and cook the vegetable crunchies for 8 minutes, turning once, until golden. Drain on paper towels.

MAKES: *8 crunchies*
PREPARATION TIME: *25 minutes*
COOKING TIME: *15 minutes*
FREEZING: *recommended*

INGREDIENTS
12 oz potato, peeled and cut in chunks
2 oz frozen mixed vegetables
1 green onion, trimmed and finely chopped
1 tablespoon smooth peanut butter
3 tablespoons milk
1 large egg
1 cup fresh white bread crumbs
1/4 cup finely grated Cheddar or Colby cheese
1 teaspoon sesame seeds
oil for frying

SERVES: *1*
PREPARATION TIME: *5 minutes*
FREEZING: *not recommended*

INGREDIENTS
1 hard boiled egg
1 teaspoon mayonnaise
1 teaspoon active-culture yogurt
1 oz carrot, grated
1 teaspoon raisins
2 lettuce leaves
alfalfa sprouts
2 cherry tomatoes, quartered
2 stuffed olives, sliced

Mimosa eggs

Hard boiled eggs are a great convenience food and a cheap source of protein. The whites are ideal containers for all manner of delicious fillings, but the yolks are high in cholesterol, so limit your child's consumption of eggs to about four a week. Serve with dark bread.

1 Cut the egg in half and mash the yolk in a small bowl, with the mayonnaise and yogurt. Stir in the carrot and raisins.
2 Arrange the lettuce leaves and alfalfa sprouts on a plate. Spoon the egg-yolk filling back into the egg whites. Place the egg-halves on top of the lettuce. Arrange the tomatoes and olives on top and serve immediately.

MAKES: *12 rolls*
PREPARATION TIME: *20 minutes*
COOKING TIME: *15 minutes*
FREEZING: *recommended*

INGREDIENTS
1/2 carrot, cut in matchsticks
1/2 small red or green pepper, seeded and cut in tiny cubes
6 snow pea pods, shredded
1 oz fresh bean sprouts
3 oz tofu, cut in small cubes
1 teaspoon tomato catsup
1 tablespoon low-sodium soy sauce
6 spring-roll wrappers
peanut oil for frying

Spring rolls

You'll find ready-made spring-roll wrappers in the supermarket's freezer section; alternatively, use filo or thinly rolled flaky pastry. Serve with soy sauce for dipping, and carrot and cucumber sticks.

1 Mix the vegetables and tofu together in a bowl. Stir in the tomato ketchup and soy sauce and allow to stand for about 30 minutes.
2 Halve each spring-roll wrapper and moisten the edge with water. Divide the filling between each wrapper and roll them up, tucking in the ends to seal the roll like a little package.
3 Heat the oil in a shallow frying pan until a cube of bread will sizzle within 30 seconds. Fry half the spring rolls over medium heat for about 8 minutes, or until golden. Drain on paper towels and keep hot while frying the second batch.

HINTS AND TIPS
Freeze uncooked spring rolls loose on a tray until firm and then wrap them in plastic wrap.

Tomato and spinach pie

This colorful, layered dish couldn't be simpler. Make it in one large or four small ramekins. Serve with vegetable sticks.

1 Preheat the oven to 375°F. Cook the spinach in a saucepan over medium heat for 5 minutes, or until wilted. Press the spinach in a colander to remove excess water.
2 Lightly oil four 6 fl oz ramekins or a 6-inch soufflé dish. Layer up the Cheddar cheese, tomatoes, spinach and potatoes, ending with a layer of potatoes.
3 Beat the eggs and milk together and then pour them over the vegetables in the dish(es). Cover with foil and bake for 1 hour, or until the potatoes are tender and the custard set.
4 Allow to cool for a few minutes in the dish and then turn the pie out on to a plate.

SERVES: *4*
PREPARATION TIME: *30 minutes*
COOKING TIME: *1 hour*
FREEZING: *not recommended*

INGREDIENTS
8 oz fresh young spinach leaves, rinsed and shredded
½ cup grated Cheddar cheese
4 firm tomatoes, thinly sliced
3 potatoes, peeled and thinly sliced
2 large eggs
2 cups milk

Peanut powerballs

Peanuts pack an awful lot of protein into a small nut, but they need to be combined with other protein-rich foods to provide all the necessary amino acids. Soya meal provides just that. Serve with tomato wedges and french fries.

1 Heat the oil in a saucepan and cook the vegetables for 5 minutes. Stir in the tomato catsup, cover and cook over low heat for 10 minutes, or until tender.
2 Blend the peanuts in a food processor until smooth. Add the cooked vegetables and rice, and blend briefly until finely chopped. Stir in half the egg and 1 oz of the bread crumbs.
3 Using moistened hands, shape the mixture into eight small balls. Coat the balls in soya meal, dip them in the remaining egg and then roll them in the remaining bread crumbs. Chill until ready to cook.
4 Preheat the oven to 425°F. Put the powerballs on a baking sheet and bake for 20 minutes, or until crisp and golden.

MAKES: *8 powerballs*
PREPARATION TIME: *20 minutes*
COOKING TIME: *35 minutes*
FREEZING: *recommended*

INGREDIENTS
2 teaspoons sunflower oil
½ small onion, peeled and finely chopped
1 celery stalk, finely chopped
1 carrot, finely cubed
1 strip each red and green pepper, seeded and chopped
2 oz green beans, trimmed and sliced
1 teaspoon tomato catsup
2 oz unsalted peanuts
¾ cup cooked brown rice
1 large egg, beaten
1½ cups whole wheat bread crumbs
2 tablespoons soya meal

LUNCH BOXES

Giving children their own lunch boxes enables you to keep control of their eating, provided, of course, that they don't swap with their friends! In this section both sweet and savory recipe ideas are provided. Try to include a high-protein and energy combination every day, plus a fruit juice drink, a piece of fruit, or fruit yogurt.

Sandwiches

The ubiquitous sandwich can be made with an infinite variety of fillings. Here I have included some of my family's favorites, plus some novel ideas of how to move beyond the usual squares or triangles.

Presentation is very important to a child. You'll soon discover they eat most of what they find attractive. Fortunately, sandwiches can come in all shapes, colors and sizes.

▲ Try using different types of bread: pita bread, dried fruit bread, nut loaves, rolls, bagels, French bread, English muffins, naan bread, or tortillas.

▲ Use cutters to shape sliced bread into little people, a favorite animal (cats and dogs always seem popular), cars, boats, trains, trucks, or any other shape.

▲ Make pinwheel sandwiches by trimming the crusts from thinly sliced bread. Roll them to flatten them and then spread the slices with the filling. Roll the bread up and slice into wheels.

▲ Make checkerboard sandwiches by using 1 white and 1 brown slice of bread. Cut off the crusts and cut the sandwiches in 1-inch squares and then fit the squares back together in a checker-board pattern, alternating brown and white squares.

▲Make polka dot sandwiches by using the end of a piping nozzle to remove ½-inch disks from 1 white and 1 brown slice of bread. Replace the white disks in the holes in the brown bread and vice versa.

▲Make open sandwiches by toasting one side of a slice of bread and topping it with filling.

▲More elaborate open sandwiches can be made by trimming away the crusts from a slice of bread and rolling the slice to flatten it somewhat. Spoon the filling diagonally across the center and then lift up opposite corners, pinch them together and fasten them together with a matchstick of carrot or cucumber.

> ### HINTS AND TIPS
> *Wrap sandwiches in plastic wrap or foil, or put them in plastic sandwich bags before packing the lunch box, to keep the sandwiches fresh. During hot weather, include a small, frozen picnic block in the lunchbox.*

SANDWICH FILLINGS

We would need a whole book to cover all the possibilities, but here are my top twenty.

Mashed avocado, lemon juice and cottage cheese

Mashed avocado, lemon juice, and frilly lettuce

Mashed banana and date spread

Mashed banana and smooth peanut butter

Cream cheese, toasted sesame seeds, and watercress

Cream cheese, toasted ground walnuts, and watercress

Cream cheese and chopped dried apricots

Grated Cheddar cheese and chopped mango chutney

Grated Cheddar cheese, tomato and corn relish

Grated Cheddar cheese, grated apple, and golden raisins

Grated Cheddar cheese and coleslaw

Hard boiled egg, mashed with mayonnaise, yogurt, and a pinch of curry powder

Hard boiled egg, mashed with mayonnaise, and cucumber

Hard boiled egg, mashed with mayonnaise and yogurt, and alfalfa sprouts

Chopped falafel with hummus and tomato

Sliced falafel with grated carrot, sesame seeds and raisins

Hummus, shredded carrot, and sliced cucumber

Yeast extract and scrambled eggs

Smoked tofu and barbecue sauce

Smoked tofu, sliced tomato, and tomato chutney

MAKES: *4 pastries*

PREPARATION TIME: *15 minutes*

CHILLING TIME: *15 minutes*

COOKING TIME: *20 minutes*

FREEZING: *not recommended*

INGREDIENTS

1 cup unbleached white flour

1 cup flour

4 oz margarine

6 oz can of baked beans in tomato sauce

2 oz each cooked navy beans and red kidney beans

1 celery stalk, trimmed and finely chopped

1 tablespoon chopped fresh cilantro

a pinch of ground cumin

a little milk

1 teaspoon poppy seeds

Cheesy bean pastries

If you have a pastry press, these can be shaped in no time; if not, use a saucer or pastry cutter as a guide for cutting out the pastry circles.

1 Sift the flours into a bowl and return any bran left in the sifter to the bowl. Cut the margarine into the flour until the mixture resembles fine breadcrumbs. Stir in enough water to form a soft, but not sticky, ball of dough.

2 Roll out the dough on a lightly floured surface. Cut out four 5-inch circles and moisten the edges. Mix together the beans, celery, coriander and cumin. Spoon an equal portion of filling into the center of each circle.

3 Lift the edges of the dough and press the edges together to seal. Put the pastries on a baking sheet, spaced a little apart, and chill them for 15 minutes. Meanwhile, preheat the oven to 400°F.

4 Brush the top of each pastry with milk and then sprinkle the poppy seeds over the top. Bake the pastries for 20 minutes or until golden.

MAKES: *6 large muffins or 12 mini-muffins*

PREPARATION TIME: *10 minutes*

COOKING TIME: *25 minutes for large muffins; 15 minutes for mini-muffins*

FREEZING: *not recommended*

INGREDIENTS

2¹/₂ cups unnbleached flour

1 tablespoon baking powder

A pinch of salt

2 large eggs

1 cup milk

¹/₂ cup or 1 stick butter or margarine, melted

Mighty muffins

These can be sweet or savory, with as simple or complex a filling as you want. I prefer them made with unbleached white flour, but for more fiber, calcium and vitamin B, make them with whole wheat flour or use a mixture of the two.

1 Preheat the oven to 400°F. Grease the muffin pan with oil. Sift the flour, baking powder and salt together. In a large bowl, beat together the eggs, milk, and melted butter or margarine. Sift in the dry ingredients.

2 Mix together gently; do not over-beat. Add your chosen flavoring and mix in lightly. Spoon the batter into the pan and cook for 20–25 minutes for large muffins, 15 minutes for mini-muffins. Cool on a wire rack.

SAVORY VARIATIONS:

Cheese and onion muffins
Fry ½ finely chopped onion in oil until golden. Allow to cool, and then add to the muffin mixture with ½ cup grated Cheddar cheese. Top with extra grated cheese before baking.

Sunshine seeds muffins
Add 2 tablespoons of sunflower seeds and ½ teaspoon of yeast extract to the muffin mixture. Sprinkle the muffins with sesame seeds before baking.

Peanut muffins
Stir 3 tablespoons of smooth peanut butter into the muffin mixture.

Carrot and mustard muffins
Grate 1 medium carrot and stir it into the muffin mixture, with 2 teaspoons of coarse-grain mustard.

SWEET VARIATIONS:

Add ⅓ cup of superfine sugar and 1 teaspoon of vanilla extract to the melted mixture in all cases.

Chocolate and raisin muffins
Coarsely chop 3 oz of plain or milk chocolate and stir into the muffin mixture, with 3 tablespoons of raisins.

Carrot and orange muffins
Grate 1 carrot and add it to the muffin mixture, with the grated zest of 1 unwaxed orange. Top with a sprinkling of sugar crystals.

Cherry and lemon muffins
Add ⅓ cup of chopped candied cherries and the grated peel of 1 small unwaxed lemon to the muffin mixture. Top with 2 tablespoons of chopped candied cherries.

Salad servings

A sneaky way to get your children to eat more greens and fiber is to give them a salad in their lunch box. Make it up in layers so they won't be bored by one taste or texture. Choose from the following:

Baby potato and chive salad
Scrub baby potatoes and cook them in their skins. While they are still warm, toss them in a mixture of mayonnaise, yogurt, and snipped chives.

Spinach and crispy bread salad
Fry cubes of bread in olive oil until crisp. Drain on paper towels. While still warm, toss with washed and dried young spinach leaves, halved cherry tomatoes and cubed cucumber.

Sprouting salad
Cube silken tofu and toss the cubes with fresh bean sprouts, grated carrot, alfalfa sprouts and finely chopped, peeled cucumber. Add a dressing made with low-sodium soy sauce, sesame oil, and fresh orange juice.

Pink ink salad
Mix together cream cheese, mayonnaise, chopped hard boiled egg, and cubed cooked beets.

Cheese and pineapple salad
Cube Cheddar cheese and mix it with fresh or canned pineapple pieces, cottage cheese, and a little yogurt.

Nuts and bolts salad
Mix together cooked red kidney beans, black eyed beans, navy beans, and corn. Cube some peeled cucumber and stir it in with some watercress. Toss in a little vinaigrette dressing.

Bar cookies

Bar cookies have become increasingly popular in the last few years, and they take so little effort to make that it is really worthwhile to make your own.

1 Lightly grease a 7-inch square shallow pan. Preheat the oven to 350°F. Melt the margarine in a saucepan with the sugar and syrup.
2 Add the oats and vanilla extract and stir well to coat. Spoon into the pan, pressing it down well with the back of a spoon. Bake for 20 minutes, or until golden.
3 Allow to cool slightly in the pan and then mark into bars and loosen the edges. When cold, remove from pan and break into bars. Store the cookies in an airtight container for up to a week. (They probably won't last that long!)

MAKES: *10 bar cookies*
PREPARATION TIME: *5 minutes*
COOKING TIME: *20 minutes*
FREEZING: *not recommended*

INGREDIENTS
3 oz stick margarine
¼ cup light brown sugar
2 tablespoons corn syrup
2 cups rolled oats
1 teaspoon vanilla extract

Mushroom rolls

These look just like sausage rolls and are made in the same way, but they are much healthier and more tasty.

1 Sift the flour into a bowl and return any bran left in the sifter to the bowl. Cut the margarine into the flour until the mixture resembles fine bread crumbs. Add enough cold water to make a soft, but not sticky, ball of dough. Wrap and chill until required.
2 Heat the olive oil in a saucepan and add the garlic and mushrooms. Cook over medium heat for 10 minutes, stirring frequently until tender. Transfer to a blender or a food processor and blend with the coriander, parsley and bread crumbs. Stir in enough egg to bind.
3 Roll out the dough on a lightly floured surface to a 12 x 8 inch rectangle. Cut in half lengthwise. Divide the filling in half and spoon half down the center of each portion of dough. Moisten the edges with water and lift the edges over the filling. Press the edges together to seal them.
4 Cut into 2-inch rolls. Place the rolls on a baking sheet spaced a little apart. Chill for 15 minutes. Preheat the oven to 400°F. Brush the rolls with milk and sprinkle them with sesame seeds. Bake for 15–20 minutes, or until golden.

MAKES: *12 rolls*
PREPARATION TIME: *35 minutes*
CHILLING TIME: *15 minutes*
COOKING TIME: *30 minutes*
FREEZING: *recommended*

INGREDIENTS
2¼ cups whole wheat flour
4 oz margarine
FOR THE FILLING:
1 tablespoon olive oil
1 garlic clove, crushed
1 lb button mushrooms, wiped and finely chopped
a pinch of ground coriander
1 tablespoon chopped fresh parsley
2 cups fresh whole wheat bread crumbs
1 large egg, beaten
2 teaspoons sesame seeds

SIDE DISHES

Simple meals can be enhanced by the addition of imaginative and complementary side dishes. They don't need to be complicated and time-consuming to prepare, and they can often be a clever way to serve vegetables appealingly (or even incognito!) to children who don't like them. Here are creative ideas for presenting faithful old potatoes; and entertaining ways to present nutritious but not always popular vegetables like carrots, cabbage and spinach.

SERVES: *4*
PREPARATION TIME: *15 minutes*
COOKING TIME: *1 hour*
FREEZING: *not recommended*

INGREDIENTS
1 lb potatoes
1/3 cup corn oil
2 teaspoons sesame oil
1 tablespoon sesame seeds

HINTS AND TIPS
Cook sweet potatoes in the same way. Allow the potatoes to cool slightly before serving to small children.

Sesame spuds

Children love the crunchy texture of these roasted potatoes. They are great with salads, or serve them as an alternative to baked potatoes.

1 Peel the potatoes and cut them in wedges. Using a sharp knife, make slits along one side, taking care not to cut right through. Put the potatoes in a saucepan and cover them with cold water. Bring the water to a boil and cook for about 10 minutes, or until tender.
2 Meanwhile, preheat the oven to 400°F. Put the corn and sesame oils into an ovenproof shallow dish. Heat the dish in the oven for 5 minutes.
3 Drain the potatoes and add them to the dish. Toss them well to coat them in the oil. Return to the oven and cook for 30 minutes. Sprinkle with the sesame seeds and cook for another 30 minutes, or until the potatoes are crisp and golden. Drain on paper towels and serve straight away.

Rösti potatoes

Less fatty than deep-fried potatoes, these little lacy potato cakes are delicious. Cook them in a mild-flavored oil, such as corn or sunflower oil.

1 Peel and coarsely grate the potato. Rinse well in a strainer until the water runs clear and then press dry in a clean dish towel.
2 Heat the oil in a large frying pan. Take about 3 tablespoons potato and put in the pan, in a little cluster. Press down slightly with the back of a fork.
3 Repeat to make about five potato cakes. Cook over medium heat for about 5 minutes, or until the underside is golden. Flip the cakes over and cook the second sides. Drain on paper towels and keep hot.
4 Cook the second batch in the same way. Serve immediately.

MAKES: *10 potato cakes*
PREPARATION TIME: *10 minutes*
COOKING TIME: *20 minutes*
FREEZING: *not recommended*

INGREDIENTS
8 oz potato
oil for frying

HINTS AND TIPS
Make a mixed vegetable rösti by grating a carrot, onion or zucchini. Mix with the potato and cook as described above.

Stuffed tomatoes

These can be prepared in advance and are very popular, because they can be eaten with just a spoon.

1 Cut the tomato(es) in half. Carefully scoop out flesh and discard the seeds. Put the chopped egg in a bowl with the tomato flesh, vegetables, mayonnaise and yogurt. Mix well.
2 Spoon the filling back in the tomato shells and sprinkle with snipped chives.

SERVES: *2*
PREPARATION TIME: *10 minutes*
FREEZING: *not recommended*

INGREDIENTS
1 large tomato or 2 small tomatoes
1 hard boiled egg, shelled and roughly chopped
1 oz mixed vegetables, cooked
1 tablespoon mayonnaise
1 teaspoon yogurt
a few snipped fresh chives

HINTS AND TIPS
Transform these into boats by making a mast from a stick of carrot and sails from a slice of cheese.

Fried rice

As rice is often a child's first food, it is not surprising how popular it becomes. Add some cooked kidney beans or extra vegetables to turn this simple side dish into a main course meal.

SERVES: *2*
PREPARATION TIME: *5 minutes*
COOKING TIME: *12 minutes*
FREEZING: *not recommended*

INGREDIENTS
3 tablespoons long-grain white rice
1 oz small frozen peas
1 oz frozen corn
1 strip red pepper, seeded and cubed
1 teaspoon sesame oil
2 teaspoons low-sodium light soy sauce
1 large egg

1 Cook the rice in boiling water for 5 minutes. Add the peas, corn and pepper and return to a boil. Cook for another 5 minutes, or until the rice and vegetables are tender. Drain the rice and vegetables well.
2 Rinse and dry the pan. Add the oil and heat it gently. Beat the soy sauce with the egg. Return the rice mixture to the pan, and, stirring continuously, add the egg.
3 Cook over high heat, stirring, until the egg has set completely. Serve immediately.

Vegetable fritters

This light batter is another great way for children to enjoy the natural taste of vegetables. The vegetables are deep-fried for only a few minutes, and retain all their goodness and flavor.

SERVES: *4*
PREPARATION TIME: *10 minutes*
COOKING TIME: *10 minutes*
FREEZING: *not recommended*

INGREDIENTS
1 cup unbleached all-purpose flour
1 tablespoon cornstarch
2 egg whites, whisked lightly
1 tablespoon low-sodium light soy sauce
peanut oil for deep-frying
4 button mushrooms, wiped
1 zucchini, cut in 1/2-inch pieces
2-inch piece of eggplant, cut in small cubes
4 broccoli flowerets
2 tomatoes, cut in wedges

1 Mix the flours together in a bowl. Make a well in the center and add the egg whites, soy sauce and enough water to give the consistency of heavy cream. Allow to stand for a few minutes.
2 Meanwhile, heat the oil in a deep pan until the temperature reaches 375°F, or when a cube of bread rises and sizzles within 30 seconds.
3 Meanwhile, add the vegetables to the batter. Mix lightly to coat the vegetables completely. Deep-fry the mushrooms and zucchini for 2–3 minutes, or until golden. Drain on paper towels. Then cook the eggplant and broccoli for about the same time. Finally, cook the tomatoes for 1–2 minutes only.

Glazed carrots

Old carrots contain more vitamin A than young ones, and what better way to use them up but in this tasty dish?

1 Put the carrots, butter or margarine, orange zest and juice and sugar in a medium-size saucepan and cook over low heat until the butter or margarine has melted.
2 Cook uncovered, stirring occasionally, for 10 minutes, or until the carrots are tender and the liquid has more or less evaporated. If desired, sprinkle with parsley before serving.

SERVES: *2*
PREPARATION TIME: *5 minutes*
COOKING TIME: *10 minutes*
FREEZING: *not recommended*

INGREDIENTS
1 large carrot, cut in sticks
1 tablespoon butter or margarine
grated zest and juice of 1 small unwaxed orange
1 teaspoon turbinado sugar

Ratatouille

The eggplant and zucchini are salted to get rid of their bitter juices. Rinse them well before you cook them, especially if you are serving this to a child under three years old.

1 Trim the eggplant and zucchini. Cut them in a child's bite-size cubes and layer them in a colander, set over a plate, with salt. Leave for 30 minutes.
2 Preheat the oven to 350°F. Rinse the eggplant and zucchini thoroughly and then dry them with paper towels. Heat the oil in a flameproof casserole and cook the onion and garlic for 5 minutes, or until softened. Add all the other vegetables and cook over medium heat for 10 minutes, stirring occasionally.
3 Stir in the tomato paste, herbs and sugar. Cover and bake for 1 hour, or until the vegetables are tender.

SERVES: 6
PREPARATION TIME: *20 minutes*
STANDING TIME: *30 minutes*
COOKING TIME: *1 hour*
FREEZING: *recommended*

INGREDIENTS
1 eggplant
2 zucchini
2 teaspoons salt
1 tablespoon olive oil
1 small onion, finely chopped
1 small garlic clove, crushed
1 each, small green and red pepper, seeded and chopped
1 lb tomatoes, skinned, seeded and chopped
1 tablespoon tomato paste
a pinch of dried mixed herbs
a pinch of soft brown sugar

HINTS AND TIPS
For a main meal, top with 2 cups fresh bread crumbs, mixed with grated cheese. Broil until golden.

SERVES: *10*
SOAKING TIME: *overnight*
PREPARATION TIME: *20 minutes*
COOKING TIME: *3½ hours*
FREEZING: *recommended*

INGREDIENTS
8 oz dried white or navy beans
1 lb tomatoes, skinned and seeded
3 tablespoons tomato paste
3 tablespoons molasses
2 teaspoons mustard powder
2 cups hot vegetable stock

HINTS AND TIPS
*Freeze single portions in empty
yogurt containers.*

Home-baked beans

Home-made baked beans bear no resemblance to the commercial canned variety. The long, slow cooking intensifies the flavor without ruining their nutritional quality. The beans are high in protein, calcium, iron, and potassium.

1 Put the beans in a large bowl and cover with cold water. Allow to soak overnight.

2 Drain the beans well. Put them in a saucepan and cover with cold water by at least 2 inches. Bring the water to a boil. Skim the surface, cover the pan and cook at a rolling boil for about 25 minutes. Drain well.

3 Preheat the oven to 300°F. Put the beans in a large casserole and stir in the tomatoes. Mix together the tomato paste, molasses, mustard and stock. Pour the stock mixture over the beans and mix well.

4 Cover the casserole and cook the beans for 2½ hours. Stir gently and cook for another 35 minutes, or until the beans are tender and the sauce thickened. Serve hot or cold.

SERVES: *8*
PREPARATION TIME: *20 minutes*
COOKING TIME: *10 minutes*
FREEZING: *recommended*

INGREDIENTS
2 lb fresh spinach leaves, washed
2 green onions, trimmed and finely chopped
2 tablespoons butter or margarine
½ cup light cream or half-and-half
a pinch of ground nutmeg

Popeye's spinach

Spinach is available all year round, and it contains a good quantity of iron and vitamin C. The young leaves are best served raw in salads, but this cooked dish adds protein, energy and vitamin D.

1 Put the spinach leaves in a large saucepan, with the green onions and butter or margarine. Cook over medium heat for 10 minutes, or until tender, stirring frequently. Drain well.

2 Return the spinach to the pan and stir in the cream and nutmeg. Reheat gently, stirring. Serve at once.

Crunchy seaweed

To tell the truth, this is not seaweed but finely shredded green cabbage. When prepared in this way, however, cabbage makes great imitation seaweed and this is actually what most Chinese restaurants serve. Children love the idea that they are eating sea greens.

1 Rinse the cabbage and dry it thoroughly in a salad spinner or clean dish towel. Heat the oil in a deep frying-pan until the temperature reaches 375°F, or when a cube of bread rises to the surface and starts to sizzle within 30 seconds of being dropped in the oil.

2 Add the cabbage and stir gently, so that all the leaves are immersed. Cook for 2 minutes.

3 Meanwhile, mix the sugar and salt together. Drain the cabbage on paper towels and sprinkle it with the seasoning mixture immediately. Serve as soon as possible.

SERVES: *4*
PREPARATION TIME: *5 minutes*
COOKING TIME: *5 minutes*
FREEZING: *not recommended*

INGREDIENTS
4 oz dark green cabbage, finely shredded
peanut oil for deep-frying
1 teaspoon granulated sugar
1/2 teaspoon sea salt

HINTS AND TIPS
Serve this with oriental-style meals, such as stir-frys or spring rolls.

Coleslaw

Most children like coleslaw, and a good thing too, because coleslaw has a generous provision of vitamins and fiber. However, it is low in protein, so serve it with something else to balance the meal. For variety and to boost the nutrients, try adding cubes of cheese, cooked red kidney beans, dried apricots, golden raisins or grated apple.

Mix all the ingredients together in a bowl. Cover and chill for 2 hours, or until required.

SERVES: 6
PREPARATION TIME: *10 minutes*
FREEZING: *not recommended*

INGREDIENTS
1/4 white cabbage, finely shredded
1 carrot, finely shredded
1/2 small onion, finely shredded
1 celery stalk, finely chopped
1 tablespoon chopped fresh parsley
1/2 cup mayonnaise
1/3 cup yogurt
salt and pepper

HINTS AND TIPS
Unlike commercially-made coleslaw, this will not keep for more than 2 days in the refrigerator.

DESSERTS

When you have a family to feed, desserts have to be quick, easy and nutritious. So here you'll find a number of ideas — from prepare-ahead puddings that can be cooked alongside the main course dish, to quick refrigerator desserts — as well as some classic favorites that, with a little adjustment, can easily fit into the healthy-eating style of today.

SERVES: *4*
PREPARATION TIME: *10 minutes*
SOAKING TIME: *30 minutes*
COOKING TIME: *1 hour*
FREEZING: *not recommended*

INGREDIENTS

6 slices of whole-grain bread
4 tablespoons butter or margarine
2 oz mixed dried fruit, e.g., figs,
  apricots, peaches, raisins,
  currants, etc.
3 tablespoons light brown sugar
2 large eggs
2 1/2 cups milk

Bread and butter pudding

A great pudding that never seems outdated. This is the ideal after-school snack to have ready on cold winter days, when the children come home starving. Its high protein, carbohydrate, and calcium content will certainly help replace the energy lost during an afterschool softball or soccer game.

1 Lightly grease an ovenproof dish. Spread the slices of bread with the butter or margarine and cut them into triangles. Layer them in the dish, with the dried fruit and sugar.
2 Preheat the oven to 325°F. Beat the eggs and milk together and pour them over the bread. Soak for 30 minutes.
3 Bake for 45 minutes to 1 hour, or until set and golden.

HINTS AND TIPS
Children love this topped with a spoonful of jam. A less sweet alternative is to use an all-fruit spread.

Knights, castles, and custard

A simple, steamed pudding that does not require close attention. Traditionally, this is made with a red-fruit jam; to reduce the sugar, choose a low-sugar fruit spread instead. Serve with custard.

1 Grease and line the bottom of four individual ramekins or cups. Using an electric mixer, beat together the margarine, sugar, flour and eggs, until smooth.

2 Divide the fruit spread equally between the cups and then spoon in the batter. Cover the tops with foil and steam for 1¼ hours, or until the puddings have risen and a knife comes out clean when you insert it.

3 To make the custard: beat the egg yolks, sugar, cornstarch and vanilla extract together. Heat the milk and then pour it into the egg mixture. Return to the pan and stir over low heat until the mixture just coats the back of a spoon.

4 Loosen the edges of the puddings and then turn them out into serving bowls. Allow to cool slightly before serving.

SERVES: *4*
PREPARATION TIME: *15 minutes*
COOKING TIME: *1¼ hours*
FREEZING: *recommended*

INGREDIENTS
½ cup soft margarine
½ cup superfine sugar
1 cup unbleached all-purpose flour
2 large eggs
⅓ cup red-fruit spread
FOR THE CUSTARD:
2 egg yolks
1 tablespoon superfine sugar
1 tablespoon cornstarch
1 teaspoon vanilla extract
2 cups milk

Rice and golden raisin pudding

To be at its best, this requires long, slow cooking, but the preparation takes practically no time at all. It is a high-energy and high-protein pudding, ideal for cold wintry days.

Preheat the oven to 300°F. Put the rice, sugar and golden raisins into a 1 quart ovenproof dish. Stir in the milk, then float the butter or margarine on top. Sprinkle with the nutmeg and cook for 2 hours, or until the rice is tender and the top is golden.

SERVES: *4*
PREPARATION TIME: *2 minutes*
COOKING TIME: *2 hours*
FREEZING: *not recommended*

INGREDIENTS
¼ cup short-grain white rice
¼ cup light brown sugar
⅓ cup golden raisins
2½ cups milk
2 tablespoons butter or margarine
a pinch of grated nutmeg

HINTS AND TIPS
For added fiber, serve this with sliced banana.

Toffee creams

SERVES: *6*
PREPARATION TIME: *15 minutes*
COOKING TIME: *1¼ hours*
CHILLING TIME: *overnight*
FREEZING: *recommended*

INGREDIENTS
½ cup granulated sugar
⅔ cup cold water
4 large eggs
2½ cups milk
½ teaspoon vanilla extract

HINTS AND TIPS
Remove from the refrigerator
30 minutes before serving.

As you would expect, this contains a fairly high amount of sugar, so it's not something to serve regularly. However, it is very high in protein, which is very important for a vegetarian child.

1 Put all but 1 tablespoon of the sugar in a saucepan with the water. Stir over low heat until all the sugar has dissolved. Increase the heat and bring to a boil. Boil steadily until the mixture turns a deep golden color.
2 Quickly pour the caramel into the bottom of each of six small ramekins or ovenproof cups. Preheat the oven to 325°F.
3 Whisk the eggs and reserved sugar together. Heat the milk and then whisk it into the eggs. Add the vanilla extract.
4 Strain the mixture into the ramekins or cups and place them in a shallow ovenproof dish. Pour in enough boiling water to come half-way up the sides of the ramekins or cups. Cook for 1 hour, or until the custard is just set and firm to the touch.
5 Remove the ramekins or cups from the dish and leave them to cool. Cover the tops with plastic wrap and chill overnight.
6 Using a round-bladed knife, loosen the edges and turn out into serving bowls. Leave upturned in the bowl for several minutes, to allow the caramel to drain out.

Surprise mice

SERVES: *2*
PREPARATION TIME: *10 minutes*
CHILLING TIME: *30 minutes*
FREEZING: *not recommended*

INGREDIENTS
2 oz (⅓ package) of lime jello
⅔ cup boiling water
1 pear
6 raisins
1 strip of red licorice string
2 white chocolate buttons, halved
1 small piece of lime peel, cut into strips

Getting your children to eat fresh pears couldn't be easier when they are transformed into little mice.

1 Make the jello with the boiling water. Add an ice cube and stir until the cube has melted. Pour a layer of jello on to two dishes and chill them until set.
2 Peel, core, and halve the pear. Place the pear-halves, cored-side down, on each jello base. Arrange the raisins for the nose and eyes, licorice for the tail, chocolate for the ears, and lime peel for whiskers.

Easy apple pie

Filo pastry contains very little fat, requires no rolling, and can be kept in the freezer. It also isn't difficult to handle and makes a delicious, crisp topping for fruit pies.

1 Preheat the oven to 400°F. Put the apples, superfine sugar, cinnamon and apple juice into a saucepan. Cook gently until the sugar has dissolved. Increase the heat and cook, stirring frequently, until the apples are soft.
2 Spoon into four individual pie dishes. Halve two sheets of filo pastry. Scrunch up one half with a whole sheet and lay them on top of the apples. Brush it with the butter and then sprinkle with sugar. Repeat with the remaining filo sheets.
3 Cook for 10–15 minutes, or until the topping is crisp and golden. Serve hot or cold.

SERVES: *4*
PREPARATION TIME: *5 minutes*
COOKING TIME: *20 minutes*
FREEZING: *not recommended*

INGREDIENTS
4 dessert apples, peeled, cored and diced
1 teaspoon superfine sugar
1/2 teaspoon ground cinnamon
1/2 cup apple juice
6 sheets of filo pastry
2 tablespoons butter or margarine, melted
2 tablespoons turbinado sugar

Teeny trifles

Trifles are perennial favorites for dessert, and this one could hardly be easier to prepare.

1 Put a slice of jelly roll into the base of four small sundae dishes. Divide the fruit between the dishes and then add the orange juice. Soak for 5 minutes and then spoon over the vanilla yogurt to cover the fruit completely.
2 Top with a dollop of sour cream or crème fraîche and decorate with chocolate strands or sprinkles before serving.

SERVES: *4*
PREPARATION TIME: *10 minutes*
FREEZING: *not recommended*

INGREDIENTS
4 slices of raspberry jelly roll
2 oz fresh or frozen raspberries
2 mandarin oranges, peeled and segmented
1/3 cup fresh orange juice
1 cup vanilla yogurt
1/3 cup sour cream or crème fraîche
chocolate strands or sprinkles, to decorate

LIGHT SUPPERS

A great selection of fun food that will tempt even the fussiest of eaters, from savory toast-toppers to make-ahead, savory cakes.

MAKES: *4*

PREPARATION TIME: *30 minutes*

CHILLING TIME: *15 minutes*

COOKING TIME: *35 minutes*

FREEZING: *recommended, for unfilled treasure chests*

INGREDIENTS

8 oz puff pastry

beaten egg to glaze

1 teaspoon sesame seeds

2 teaspoons soft margarine

2 teaspoons unbleached all-purpose flour

2/3 cup milk

1 oz American or Swiss cheese, grated

1 tablespoon smooth peanut butter

3 tablespoons frozen mixed vegetables

2 oz frozen corn, thawed

Treasure chests

You can fill the little puff-pastry cases with whatever your child finds most appealing. I find this a great recipe for using up leftover vegetables which are transformed by the nutty, cheesy sauce.

1 Roll out the pastry to about ⅛ inch thick. Cut out four 3 × 1 inch rectangles. Space them a little apart on a baking sheet. Re-roll the trimmings and cut out four "lids." Place them on the baking sheet.

2 Using a small, sharp knife, make a criss-cross pattern on the lids. Then, taking care not to cut right through, mark a border ¼ inch from the edge of each rectangle. Chill for 15 minutes.

3 Meanwhile, preheat the oven to 425°F. Brush the lids and the borders with egg and bake for 10 minutes, or until they have risen and are golden. Carefully press the center of each treasure chest to create a cavity.

4 Melt the margarine in a small pan and stir in the flour. Gradually add the milk and stir over medium heat until thickened. Stir in the cheese, peanut butter and mixed vegetables. Spoon the filling into the treasure chests, spoon a little corn for "gold" on top and then put on the lids. Put on serving plates and spoon the remaining "gold" around each.

Sandwich snails

These cute sandwiches can be made with a variety of fillings. For best results, use one that will spread easily.

1 Remove the crusts from the bread. Place the bread on a board, overlapping the ends slightly, and then roll them together with a rolling pin, to seal the ends and flatten the slices.
2 Mix together the cream cheese, mayonnaise, corn and pepper. Spread over the bread to cover it completely. Starting at a narrower end, roll up the bread like a jelly roll.
3 Slice in half to create two smaller rolls.
4 Place a carrot-half, rounded-side up, on each plate, and position a sandwich on top. Cut four antennae and two mouths from a piece of cucumber. Fix the antennae and mouths in place. Arrange the lettuce around the base of the snail, for grass.

MAKES: *2 snails*
PREPARATION TIME: *10 minutes*
FREEZING: *not recommended*

INGREDIENTS
2 slices of white or whole wheat bread
1/4 cup cream cheese
1 teaspoon mayonnaise
2 oz corn
1 strip of red pepper, cut in tiny cubes
1 long carrot, trimmed, peeled and halved length-wise
cucumber for the antennae and mouth
shredded lettuce for the grass

Moonbeams

Yeast extract contains all the B vitamins, as well as giving good old french toast a taste lift. Serve with wedges of apple.

1 Remove the crusts from the bread. Using a cookie cutter, cut out half-moon shapes and spread each with yeast extract.
2 Beat the egg and milk together on a plate. Dip the moonbeams in the egg mixture to coat them. Meanwhile, melt the margarine in a non-stick frying pan. Fry the moonbeams over medium heat for 2–3 minutes on each side, until golden.

SERVES: *1*
PREPARATION TIME: *5 minutes*
COOKING TIME: *5 minutes*
FREEZING: *not recommended*

INGREDIENTS
2 slices of white or whole wheat bread
1/4 teaspoon yeast extract
1 large egg
1/4 cup milk
1 teaspoon margarine

> **HINTS AND TIPS**
> *For a sweet version, use fruit spread in place of yeast extract. If you don't have a cutter, use a small sharp knife and cut the moonbeams freehand.*

Fun fingers

As tofu has such a bland flavor, it will absorb other tastes quite readily. Serve these fingers with canned spaghetti hoops in tomato sauce and Rösti Potatoes (see page 95).

MAKES: *4 fingers*
STANDING TIME: *30 minutes*
PREPARATION TIME: *20 minutes*
COOKING TIME: *10 minutes*
FREEZING: *not recommended*

INGREDIENTS
6 oz tofu in one piece
4 teaspoons low-sodium light soy sauce
¹/₂ teaspoon sesame oil
1 large egg
1 ¹/₂ cups fresh white bread crumbs
1 tablespoon sesame seeds
corn oil for frying

1 Cut the tofu into equal-sized fingers and put them in a shallow dish. Mix together the soy sauce and sesame oil and pour over the tofu. Allow to soak for about 30 minutes.
2 Beat the egg on a plate. On a second plate, mix together the bread crumbs and sesame seeds. Dip the tofu fingers in the egg, then coat them in the breadcrumbs and sesame seeds.
3 Heat a little oil in a non-stick frying pan and, turning the fingers, cook them for 4–5 minutes on each side, or until the coating is crisp and golden.

Muffin clock

You can use half a toasted English muffin or a large bread roll for these pizza-like snacks.

SERVES: *1*
PREPARATION TIME: *15 minutes*
COOKING TIME: *5 minutes*
FREEZING: *recommended*

INGREDIENTS
1 English muffin half, toasted
2 teaspoons tomato catsup
¹/₄ small green pepper, seeded
¹/₂ small yellow pepper, seeded
¹/₂ oz slice of cheddar cheese
2 slices of tiny button mushrooms

1 Preheat the broiler. Spread the muffin half with tomato catsup to cover it completely. Using small number cookie-cutters, stamp out 12, 3, 6 and 9 from the green pepper. Then stamp out 1, 2, 4, 5, 7, 8, 10 and 11 from the yellow pepper. Position on the muffin half.
2 Using a sharp knife, cut clock "hands" from the cheese and place on the pizza. Fix the mushrooms at the end of the "hands."
3 Brush the vegetables with a little oil and broil for 5 minutes, or until the cheese is bubbling. Allow to cool slightly before serving.

> **HINTS AND TIPS**
> *For a party, make a big pizza clock using an 8-inch pizza base.*

Smiley clown

This will certainly bring a smile at supper. The hummus provides the perfect base for the clown's face, plus a fair helping of protein. Serve with breadsticks.

1 On a 7-inch plate, spread the hummus in a thin round, using a spatula if possible.

2 Arrange the features as follows: cherry tomato for the nose, alfalfa sprouts for the hair, hard boiled egg and crossed strips of green pepper for the eyes and a wedge of cheese for the mouth.

3 Shape a bow tie from the carrot and put it in place.

SERVES: *1*
PREPARATION TIME: *10 minutes*
FREEZING: *not recommended*

INGREDIENTS
2 tablespoons hummus
1/2 cherry tomato
alfalfa sprouts
2 slices of hard boiled egg
4 matchstick strips of green pepper
a small wedge of Edam cheese
1 long slice of carrot

Double deckers

Club sandwiches make quite a meal, and can be filled with whatever you happen to have in the refrigerator. Remember to remove the cocktail sticks before giving these to small children.

1 Spread one slice of bread with peanut butter and the other with cream cheese. Arrange the lettuce, cucumber and tomato on top of one slice, and then sandwich the first slice of bread together with the second slice.

2 Cut the sandwich into triangles. Stand the triangles upright on a plate and fix them together with cocktail sticks.

SERVES: *1*
PREPARATION TIME: *10 minutes*
FREEZING: *not recommended*

INGREDIENTS
2 slices of white or whole wheat bread
1 teaspoon smooth peanut butter
1 tablespoon cream cheese
2 frilly lettuce leaves
5 slices of cucumber
1 tomato, thinly sliced

Spotty dogs

The vegetarian hot dog couldn't be simpler. Use a quantity of home-baked beans and ready-made vegetarian hot dogs for a filling and fast supper.

1 Cook the hot dogs until golden and cooked through. Meanwhile, heat the beans.

2 Spoon the beans into the bun. Place the hot dogs on top, and top with the catsup. Cut in half to serve.

SERVES: *1*
PREPARATION TIME: *5 minutes*
COOKING TIME: *10 minutes*
FREEZING: *not recommended*

INGREDIENTS
2 vegetarian hot dogs
1 quantity Home-baked Beans (see page 98)
1 white or whole wheat hot dog bun
1 teaspoon tomato catsup

SERVES: *1*
PREPARATION TIME: *5 minutes*
COOKING TIME: *12 minutes*
FREEZING: *not recommended*

INGREDIENTS
1 ear of corn on the cob
1 teaspoon butter or margarine,
    melted
½ teaspoon maple syrup

Broiled corn cobs

These can be cooked in the broiler or on an outdoor grill. Serve with crusty bread and tomato wedges.

1 Preheat the broiler. Remove the outer husks and the silk from the corn cob. Brush with the melted butter or margarine and the maple syrup.
2 Cook under the broiler, turning occasionally and brushing the cob with the melted mixture until the corn kernels turn a deep golden color. Allow to cool slightly before serving.

SERVES: *2*
PREPARATION TIME: *5 minutes*
COOKING TIME: *5 minutes*
FREEZING: *recommended*

INGREDIENTS
2 oz Cheddar cheese, grated
1 small apple, grated
1 teaspoon chutney
2 slices of whole wheat bread,
    toasted

Cheesy toast squares

A de luxe version of ordinary cheese on toast. The grated apple adds vitamins and fiber as well as flavor.

1 Preheat the broiler to high. Mix together the cheese, apple and chutney. Spread an equal amount over each slice of toast to cover it completely.
2 Broil for 5 minutes, or until the topping is golden and bubbling.

HINTS AND TIPS
Make a larger quantity of the cheesy paste than you need and store the extra in single-portion sizes in the freezer. Unfrozen paste will keep for up to 2 days.

Tic-tac-toe

Use any mild-flavored cheese that melts easily for this recipe. There is no need to butter the toast, because the cheese will provide enough fat. This is a fun supper for your youngster to enjoy with a friend.

1 Preheat the broiler. Arrange the cheese on the toast to cover it completely. Arrange the beans in a grid on top. Halve the tomatoes and position them on top for "O"s. Cut the pepper strips into equal lengths and arrange them on the grid for "X"s.
2 Broil for 3–4 minutes, or until the cheese has melted and is bubbling. Allow to cool a little before serving.

SERVES: *2*
PREPARATION TIME: **5 minutes**
COOKING TIME: *3–4 minutes*
FREEZING: *not recommended*

INGREDIENTS
2 slices of whole wheat bread, toasted
8 thin slices of mozzarella cheese
8 cooked green beans
4 cherry tomatoes
4 thin matchstick strips of yellow pepper

Mexican beans

Use a portion of home-made baked beans or a selection of canned beans for this.

1 Put the beans in a saucepan, with the corn, pepper, catsup and cumin. Heat gently until the vegetables are tender.
2 Put the tortillas on a plate and pile the bean mixture on to each. Sprinkle with the cheese and serve immediately.

SERVES: *1*
PREPARATION TIME: *10 minutes*
COOKING TIME: *5 minutes*
FREEZING: *not recommended*

INGREDIENTS
1 portion Home-baked Beans (see page 98)
1 oz corn
1 strip of green pepper, seeded and diced
1 teaspoon tomato catsup
a pinch of ground cumin
3 tortillas
1/4 cup grated Cheddar cheese

SPECIAL TREATS

Make these as treats, rather than serving them every day. During the week, fresh fruit or yogurt will satisfy even the heartiest appetite.

MAKES: *16 cakes*
PREPARATION TIME: *30 minutes*
COOKING TIME: *45 minutes*
FREEZING: *recommended*

INGREDIENTS
½ cup soft margarine
½ cup light brown sugar
1 cup self-rising whole wheat flour
½ teaspoon baking powder
½ teaspoon ground cinnamon
2 large eggs
6 oz carrots, grated
grated peel and juice of 1 small unwaxed orange
FOR THE TOPPING:
⅓ cup cream cheese
⅓ cup confectioner's sugar

Frosted carrot cake

Carrot cake is a favorite with all ages. Carrots make a really moist cake and sweeten it, so you don't need much sugar.

1 Preheat the oven to 350°F. Grease and line the bottom of an 8-inch, shallow, square cake pan. Cream the margarine and sugar until they are pale and fluffy. Sift the flour, baking powder, and cinnamon together.
2 Beat the eggs into the creamed mixture and then fold in the flour and carrots. Stir in all but ½ teaspoon of the grated orange peel and all the juice. Spoon the cake batter into a pan and level the surface with the back of a spoon. Bake for 45 minutes, or until the cake is well risen and golden, and a toothpick comes out clean when you insert it in the center. Cool on a wire rack.
3 To make the topping, cream together the cream cheese and the confectioner's sugar until the mixture is fluffy. Stir in the reserved orange peel. Spread the topping over the cake and then cut into squares.

HINTS AND TIPS
For children over five years old, scatter finely chopped walnuts over the top.

Lemon ladies and men

I tend to use a basic shortbread rather than a gingerbread mix for these cookies, as it produces a nicer, more crumbly texture, which children seem to prefer.

1 Lightly grease two baking sheets. Cream together the butter and sugar until pale. Stir in the lemon peel and the flours, and mix to form a stiff dough. Knead lightly.

2 Roll out the dough on a lightly floured surface and, using gingerbread man and woman cutters, cut out the shapes. Place them, spaced a little apart, on baking sheets. Fix the raisins or currants for eyes and buttons. Mark a mouth with the tip of a knife.

3 Chill for 30 minutes. Meanwhile, preheat the oven to 350°F. Bake the cookies for 15 minutes, or until golden. Cool slightly on the baking sheet and then transfer to a wire rack. Store for up to 1 week in an airtight container.

MAKES: *about 12 people*
PREPARATION TIME: *10 minutes*
CHILLING TIME: *30 minutes*
COOKING TIME: *15–20 minutes*
FREEZING: *recommended*

INGREDIENTS
1/2 cup butter or margarine
1/4 cup superfine sugar
grated peel of 1 small unwaxed lemon
1 cup unbleached all-purpose flour
1/2 cup cornstarch
raisins or currants, to decorate

Date bars

These do not contain processed sugar; all the sweetness is provided by the dates. For a special occasion, top the bars with 2 oz of melted chocolate or carob before you cut them.

1 Preheat the oven to 350°F. Grease a 7-inch shallow square pan. Put the dates and apple juice into a saucepan and bring the juice to a boil. Reduce the heat, cover the pan and simmer for 5 minutes.

2 Remove the pan from the heat and allow the dates to cool slightly. Stir in the remaining ingredients and mix well. Pour mixture into the pan and level the surface with the back of a spoon. Cook for 30 minutes, or until the mixture begins to shrink from the sides of the pan.

3 Allow to cool in the pan for a few miinutes. Then turn out and cool on a wire rack. Cut into bars when cooled.

MAKES: *16 bars*
PREPARATION TIME: *10 minutes*
COOKING TIME: *30 minutes*
FREEZING: *recommended*

INGREDIENTS
8 oz dates, rinsed, dried and coarsely chopped
2/3 cup unsweetened apple juice
2 oz ground walnuts
1/2 cup soft margarine
1 cup whole wheat flour
2 oz oats
1 large egg

PARTY FOOD

*A birthday party means treats; this section
provides the right balance between
"healthy" and indulgent dishes. For
toddlers' birthdays keep the food to
just three or four dishes. Under the
age of four, most children will be
more concerned with presents and
games than with food, and, remember,
it is a day you all want to enjoy, so
don't make life more difficult for
yourself than you need.*

MAKES: *8 people*
PREPARATION TIME: *20 minutes*
FREEZING: *not recommended*

INGREDIENTS
*4 thin slices of unbleached white or
    whole wheat bread
a little margarine for spreading
4 thin slices of Cheddar or Colby
    cheese
red and green pepper, carrot, and
    watercress for decoration*

HINTS AND TIPS
*Cover with plastic wrap to prevent
the people from drying out.*

Birthday people

***This recipe makes eight of these little open sandwiches but be sure
to make enough for every party guest.***

1 Using a small gingerbread man and woman cutter, stamp out four
of each from the bread. Spread with margarine. Using the cutter as
a guide, cut out shirts and pants for the men, and dresses for the
ladies from the cheese. Put the clothes in place.
2 For the men, use strips of carrot for suspenders and belts, and a
little green pepper for bow ties.
3 Use red pepper to shape frilly collars and cuffs for the ladies. Put
the sandwiches on a serving plate and attach watercress for eyes and
noses, and red pepper for mouths.

Sesame snaps

These go quickly and can be cut out in fun shapes or rounds.

1 Lightly grease two baking sheets with oil. Rub the butter into the flour until the mixture resembles fine crumbs. Stir in the yeast extract, 2 teaspoons of the sesame seeds, and the cheese. Knead together to form a soft dough.

2 Roll out on a lightly floured surface and stamp out shapes with your chosen cutter. Put the shapes on a baking sheet, spaced a little apart, and prick them with a fork. Sprinkle them with the remaining sesame seeds and chill for 15 minutes.

3 Preheat the oven to 350°F. Bake the sesame snaps for 15 minutes, or until firm. Let them cool on the baking sheet for a few minutes and then transfer them to a wire rack. Once cold, store in an airtight container for up to a week.

Makes: *about 20 biscuits*
Preparation time: *10 minutes*
Chilling time: *15 minutes*
Cooking time: *15 minutes*
Freezing: *recommended*

Ingredients
1 ³⁄4 cups whole wheat flour
4 oz butter or stick margarine
¹⁄2 teaspoon yeast extract
1 tablespoon sesame seeds, toasted
¹⁄2 cup grated Cheddar cheese

Apple chips

A novel and much healthier version of much-loved potato chips.

1 Peel, core and quarter the apples. Cut each quarter into very thin slices. Do not rinse.

2 Meanwhile, heat the oil in a deep fryer until the temperature reaches 375°F, or when a cube of bread rises and sizzles within 30 seconds. Cook the apple slices in four batches for 3–4 minutes, or until the apples are crisp and golden.

3 Drain on paper towels and sprinkle with a little sugar, if desired.

Serves: *8*
Preparation time: *20 minutes*
Cooking time: *10 minutes*
Freezing: *not recommended*

Ingredients
1 lb firm apples
oil for frying
1 tablespoon superfine sugar
  (optional)

> **Hints and tips**
> *Superfine sugar mixed with a little ground cinnamon is a tasty alternative to sugar only.*

PREPARATION TIME: *15 minutes*
COOKING TIME: *according to*
    size of pan
FREEZING: *recommended*

INGREDIENTS
For every 2¹/₂ cups:
4 tablespoons soft margarine
¹/₄ cup superfine sugar
1 large egg
¹/₂ cup self-rising unbleached flour

Basic birthday cake

A simple, all-in-one cake mixture that you can adapt to suit any size or shape of cake pan. To calculate the amount of cake batter needed for your pan, fill the pan with water to the depth you want the cake to be (not right to the top of the pan). For every 2¹/₂ cups the pan holds, allow the following quantities and multiply them as required.

1 Preheat the oven to 350°F. Grease the pan and line the bottom with wax paper. Put all the ingredients into a bowl, and, using an electric mixer, beat them until smooth.
2 Spoon the mixture into the pan, level the surface with the back of a spoon and bake for the required time. As a guide, a 4-egg mixture made in two 8-inch pans will take about 35 minutes. It is difficult to give accurate timings for oddly shaped cakes, such as numerals or novelty pans, because the more contact the mixture has with the sides of the pan, the faster it will cook. Don't use this mixture for cake pans more than 10 inches at their widest point, or the edges will overcook long before the middle is ready.

FLAVORINGS

Lemon or Orange cake
Use unwaxed fruit and add the grated peel of 1 fruit to the cake batter.

Chocolate or Carob cake
Replace ¼ cup of the flour with the same amount of cocoa or carob powder.

Marble cake
Put half the cake mixture into a clean bowl and color one half as desired, using vegetable food-coloring paste. Place alternate spoonfuls of plain and colored batter in the pan, and swirl them gently together with a skewer.

Vanilla buttercream

This can be made with butter or margarine and is perhaps the simplest of fillings or frostings for a cake. For more elaborate decorations, it can be piped as well.

Cream the butter or margarine until pale. Gradually beat in the confectioner's sugar, water, and vanilla extract. Cover and chill until required. Allow to soften at room temperature before using.

FLAVORINGS

Chocolate or Carob buttercream
Dissolve 1 tablespoon cocoa or carob powder in 2 teaspoons hot water and then stir the mixture into the buttercream.

Orange or Lemon buttercream
Replace the vanilla extract with the grated peel from 1 unwaxed fruit.

MAKES: *enough to fill and coat the top of an 8-inch cake*
PREPARATION TIME: *10 minutes*
FREEZING: *not recommended*

INGREDIENTS
6 oz softened butter or margarine
2½ cups confectioner's sugar, sifted
1 tablespoon hot water
1 teaspoon vanilla extract

Fondant icing

This is not too tricky to make, and it is easy enough for even the novice in cake decorating to produce an attractive effect. If you can roll out pastry, you can ice a cake with this icing. There are some excellent brands of fondant available today, but here is a recipe for home-made fondant. You'll find liquid glucose in a jar at pharmacies or health food stores.

1 Sift the confectioner's sugar twice. Put the liquid glucose, egg white, and rosewater into a large bowl. Gradually stir in the confectioner's sugar. When the confectioner's icing is too stiff to stir, knead in the remaining confectioner's sugar by hand until the icing is completely smooth.
2 Knead until the mixture forms a soft ball. Add more confectioner's sugar if the icing remains sticky. Wrap in plastic wrap and place in a plastic bag. Store in the refrigerator.

MAKES: *450 g (1 lb)*
PREPARATION TIME: *10 minutes*
FREEZING: *recommended*

INGREDIENTS
1 lb confectioner's sugar
1 rounded tablespoon liquid glucose
1 large egg white
1 teaspoon rosewater

HINTS AND TIPS
Keep the fondant tightly covered, or it will dry out quickly and crack.

Birthday lagoon

SERVES: *8*
PREPARATION TIME: *30 minutes*
FREEZING: *not recommended*

INGREDIENTS
4 ripe avocados
3 tablespoons lemon juice
6 oz cream cheese
1 tablespoon mayonnaise
cauliflower flowerets, cucumber sticks
    and shapes, multi-colored
    peppers, breadsticks, and crackers,
    to serve

A simple avocado dip is transformed into a stunning centerpiece that requires hardly any effort to make.

1 Using three sheets of aluminum foil, shape a 12-inch shallow lagoon, and place it on a tray or a flat plate larger than the lagoon.
2 Halve each avocado and remove the pits. Scoop the flesh into a bowl and mash it with the lemon juice, cream cheese, and mayonnaise until smooth. Spoon into the lagoon, and, using a fork, spread the dip to form "waves."
3 Arrange the vegetables around the lagoon to resemble trees and flowers. Use the breadsticks and crackers for rocks. Serve immediately.

No-bake cherry crackles

MAKES: *12 crackles*
PREPARATION TIME: *10 minutes*
COOKING TIME: *5 minutes*
CHILLING TIME: *1 hour*
FREEZING: *not recommended*

INGREDIENTS
8 oz carob bar, broken into squares
1 tablespoon light corn syrup
2 oz (½ stick) butter or margarine
2 oz red candied cherries, chopped
2 oz cornflakes, coarsely crushed

You don't even have to put the oven on for these, and as they are so simple you can get the little ones to help.

1 Set 12 paper cup-cake cups on a baking sheet. Melt the carob bar, syrup and butter or margarine together, in a bowl set over a pan of simmering water.
2 Stir in the cherries and cornflakes, and then divide the mixture equally between the cup-cake cups. Chill until set.

Orange boats

A child's party just wouldn't be a party without jello, so make your own with natural fruit juice, a vegetarian setting agent like Gelozone, and a little sugar.

1 Halve each orange, and, using a teaspoon, scoop out the flesh. Take care not to pierce the skin. Wash each orange shell and reserve it. Press the flesh through a strainer and collect the juice in a jug. Make up to 2½ cups of orange juice.

2 Pour the orange juice into a saucepan and add the sugar. Sprinkle in the gelatin and then stir over low heat until dissolved. Allow to cool slightly.

3 Place the orange shells on a baking sheet and pour in the gelatin. Chill until completely set. Put on a serving plate and place a scoop of ice cream on top. Fix a wafer "sail" in place before serving.

MAKES: *8 boats*
PREPARATION TIME: *30 minutes*
CHILLING TIME: *at least 2 hours*
FREEZING: *not recommended*

INGREDIENTS
4 oranges
2 teaspoons superfine sugar
1½ teaspoons plain vegetarian gelatin
8 scoops of Home-made Vanilla Ice Cream (see page 119)
4 ice cream wafers, halved diagonally

Traffic-light Popsicles

Popsicles are a great treat, and perfect for a summer party, when they can be served outside. Make them with natural fruit juice, at least a day in advance.

1 Pour the cranberry and raspberry juice into the bottom of eight 3 fl oz popsicle molds. Freeze until solid. Top with the orange juice and freeze again, until solid.

2 Make up the limeade with the water and color it pale green if necessary. Pour into the molds and clip a popsicle stick in place. Freeze until solid. To unmold the popsicles, immerse them in hot water for 10 seconds only.

MAKES: *8 lollies*
PREPARATION TIME: *20 minutes*
FREEZING TIME: *allow at least 24 hours*

INGREDIENTS
1 cup each cranberry and raspberry juice, and orange juice
¼ cup lime cordial
¾ cup water
green natural food coloring, if necessary

HINTS AND TIPS
Set a whole fresh strawberry or raspberry in the bottom of the popsicle mold in the red fruit juice.

SERVES: *8*
PREPARATION TIME: *5 minutes*
COOKING TIME: *5 minutes*
FREEZING: *not recommended*

INGREDIENTS
½ cup corn oil
6 oz popping corn
⅓ cup maple or light corn syrup

Popcorn

A great low-fat food that children love. Popcorn is ideal for giving away in decorative wrappers as party favors.

1 Heat half the oil in a large, deep, heavy-bottomed saucepan. Add half the popping corn to the pan. Cover with a tightly-fitting lid, and then shake the pan. Cook over medium heat for 5 minutes. Shake the pan occasionally as the corn begins to pop.
2 Tip the popcorn into a large bowl and repeat with the remaining oil and corn. Warm the syrup and pour it over the popcorn. Mix well to coat the popcorn evenly.

MAKES: *12 buttercups*
PREPARATION TIME: *30 minutes*
COOKING TIME: *20 minutes*
FREEZING: *recommended*

INGREDIENTS
12 thin slices of white or whole wheat bread
⅓ cup melted butter or margarine
2 green onions, finely chopped
1 strip of green pepper, seeded and cut in small cubes
2 oz corn
3 tablespoons unbleached all-purpose flour
1¼ cups milk
½ cup grated Cheddar cheese

Cheese buttercups

Use butter or margarine to coat these little cups.

1 Preheat the oven to 400°F. Using a 3-inch flower cutter or a plain cutter, stamp out 12 shapes from the bread. Brush a 12-section muffin pan with melted butter or margarine and then press in the shapes. Brush them well with more melted butter to coat.
2 Bake for 10 minutes, or until crisp and golden. Brush with butter during baking, if some patches appear paler than the rest.
3 Add the vegetables to the remaining melted butter and cook over medium heat for 5 minutes, or until softened. Add the flour and then gradually stir in the milk. Stir over medium heat until the sauce is thickened and smooth. Add half the cheese.
4 Divide the mixture between the bread cups and sprinkle the remaining cheese on top. Cook for 5 minutes, or until the cheese has melted. Serve hot or cold.

HINTS AND TIPS
Freeze the unfilled bread cups and filling separately.

Home-made vanilla ice cream

This is just what it says, real ice cream — not the synthetic combination of fat, sugar, coloring and flavoring found in most commercial brands. Serve with puréed strawberries.

1 Put a freezer container into the freezer. Heat the milk and vanilla stick until the milk is almost boiling, then remove the pan from the heat and allow the milk to sit for 1 hour.
2 Beat the egg yolks and sugar together until thick. Remove the vanilla stick from the milk and gradually beat the milk into the egg-yolk mixture. Return the mixture to the pan and stir it over very low heat until the mixture just coats the back of a wooden spoon. Do not let it boil.
3 Pour the mixture into the chilled container and allow to cool. Seal the lid and freeze for 2 hours, or until the ice cream is just beginning to become mushy.
4 Lightly whip the cream until soft peaks form. Using an electric mixer, beat the frozen milk mixture until smooth. Fold in the cream, seal the lid again and freeze for another 2 hours.
5 Beat with an electric mixer until smooth. Then freeze overnight.

MAKES: *about 1 quart*
PREPARATION TIME: *20 minutes*
STANDING TIME: *1 hour*
FREEZING TIME: *4 hours during preparation, then overnight*

INGREDIENTS
2½ cups whole milk
1 vanilla stick
6 large egg yolks
¾ cup superfine sugar
2½ cups fresh whipping cream

HINTS AND TIPS
Allow the ice cream to soften in the refrigerator for 30 minutes before serving.

FLAVORINGS

Chocolate ice cream
Fold in 6 oz of chocolate chips with the cream.

Fruit ice cream
Purée 12 oz of fruit (e.g. strawberry, raspberry, peach), with ¼ cup confectioner's sugar, and stir the purée into the milk mixture before the first freezing stage.

MEALS IN A HURRY

There will always be the occasion when you are expected to feed them quickly, so keep a basic store cupboard of dried pasta, canned beans, soups, and sauces; coupled with a few fresh ingredients these will enable you to rustle up a nourishing meal in minutes.

SERVES: *1*
PREPARATION TIME: *10 minutes*
COOKING TIME: *5 minutes*
FREEZING: *not recommended*

INGREDIENTS

1 oz cracked wheat
2/3 cup hot vegetable stock
1 small orange, peeled and segmented
1 oz golden raisins
1 green onion, trimmed and finely chopped
1/2 celery stalk, trimmed and chopped
2 tablespoons French dressing

HINTS AND TIPS
Older children may like the addition of toasted almonds, to add crunch and protein.

Cracked wheat and orange salad

Cracked wheat adds bulk and vitamins to this simple salad. Try using cooked brown rice if you don't have any cracked wheat. Serve with pita bread.

1 Soak the cracked wheat in the vegetable stock for about 10 minutes until all the liquid is absorbed. Spoon into a heatproof colander, cover and steam over a pan of simmering water for 10 minutes, or until the wheat grains are tender.
2 Meanwhile, mix together the orange, golden raisins, green onion and celery. Add the cracked wheat and pour the dressing on while it is still warm.

Quick cannelloni

Ground walnuts add protein and flavor, but the flavor may be a little bitter if the walnuts have been stored for some time, so check the package date before using them.

1 Cook the cannelloni in boiling water for 10 minutes, or until tender. Meanwhile, mix together the cottage cheese, ground walnuts, garlic, parsley and lemon peel.
2 Preheat the broiler. Drain the cannelloni, and, using a spoon or piping bag, fill each tube with the cheese mixture. Put the tubes in a heatproof dish and spoon the tomatoes over the top.
3 Cook under the broiler until bubbling. Lay the cheese slices on top and cook for 2–3 minutes, or until melted and starting to turn golden. Make sure your child knows that cooked cheese can be very hot, though.

SERVES: *1*
PREPARATION TIME: *10 minutes*
COOKING TIME: *15 minutes*
FREEZING: *not recommended*

INGREDIENTS
2 cannelloni tubes
1/2 cup cottage cheese
1/4 cup ground walnuts
1/2 garlic clove, crushed
2 teaspoons chopped fresh parsley
grated peel of 1/2 unwaxed small lemon
1/2 a 7 oz can of chopped tomatoes
2 slices of mozzarella cheese

Spanish omelet

Any combination of vegetables can be called a Spanish omelet. Instantly satisfying, this will feed one, two, or four, depending on their appetites. Serve with a salad of lettuce wedges and fresh tomatoes.

1 Heat the oil in a non-stick 7-inch frying pan. Add the potatoes and onions and cook for 5 minutes over medium heat. Add the peas, corn and peppers and cook for 5 minutes. Drain off the excess oil.
2 Beat the eggs with 1 tablespoon water and pour them over the vegetables. Cook over medium heat for 5 minutes, or until the eggs are set. Preheat the broiler.
3 Cook the top under the broiler for a few minutes, until golden.

SERVES: *2*
PREPARATION TIME: *5 minutes*
COOKING TIME: *15 minutes*
FREEZING: *not recommended*

INGREDIENTS
1/4 cup olive oil
1 large potato, peeled and cut into 1/2-inch cubes
1 onion, peeled and finely chopped
1 oz peas
1 oz corn
1/2 small red and green pepper, seeded and chopped
4 large eggs

HINTS AND TIPS
Other vegetables, such as mushrooms, tomatoes or cooked spinach can be used.

Harlequin macaroni

The bright colors of the special mixed vegetables — and their cute little square shapes — give this recipe its name. The vegetables also add precious vitamins to the classic and nutritious combination of pasta and cheese sauce.

SERVES: *1*
PREPARATION TIME: *10 minutes*
COOKING TIME: *10 minutes*
FREEZING: *not recommended*

INGREDIENTS

1½ oz elbow macaroni
2 oz frozen mixed vegetables
1 tablespoon butter or margarine
1 tablespoon unbleached all-purpose
   flour
⅔ cup milk
1 oz cheddar or American cheese,
   grated

1 Cook the macaroni in boiling water for 6 minutes. Add the vegetables, return to boiling, and cook for 4 minutes, or until the pasta and vegetables are tender.
2 Meanwhile, melt the butter or margarine in a saucepan. Stir in the flour, then gradually add the milk. Stir over medium heat until thickened. Drain the pasta and vegetables and stir them into the sauce, with half the cheese.
3 Spoon into a serving bowl and serve with the remaining cheese.

Crunchy cheese salad

Olive oil has a mild distinct flavour; among many of its wonderful attributes it is low in polyunsaturated fat. The moist centre of grated cheese and carrot, means that dressing is not necessary for this salad.

SERVES: *1*
PREPARATION TIME: *10 minutes*
COOKING TIME: *5 minutes*
FREEZING: *not recommended*

INGREDIENTS

15 ml (1 tablespoon) olive oil
1 slice of white bread, cubed
1 Little Gem lettuce, trimmed and
   cut in wedges
1 tomato, cut in wedges
2.5 cm (1-inch) piece of cucumber,
   halved and thickly sliced
45 g (1½ oz) carrot, grated
45 g (1½ oz) Cheddar cheese,
   grated

1 Heat the oil in a non-stick frying-pan. Add the bread and fry it over a medium heat until it's golden and crisp on all sides. Drain on kitchen paper.
2 Arrange the wedges of lettuce and tomato and the cucumber slices alternately around the edge of a serving plate. Put the grated carrot and cheese in the centre and sprinkle the croûtons on top.

Tomato piperade

A colorful egg stew that, like Spanish Omelet, can be adapted to make use of whatever vegetables you have available. Serve with crusty bread or toast to mop up the vegetable juices.

1 Heat the olive oil in a saucepan and cook the onion until golden. Seed and chop the tomato and pepper strips. Add the garlic, peppers, and tomatoes and cook for 15 minutes, until the vegetables have softened to a thick pulp.
2 Beat the eggs and add them to the pan. Stir over a low heat for 5 minutes, or until the eggs are set and creamy.

SERVES: *1*
PREPARATION TIME: *10 minutes*
COOKING TIME: *20 minutes*
FREEZING: *not recommended*

INGREDIENTS
2 teaspoons olive oil
1/4 onion, finely chopped
1/2 garlic clove, crushed
3 strips of pepper
2 tomatoes, skinned
1 large egg

Fasta pasta

This can be cooked in one pan, saving on time, space and cleaning. Serve with herb or garlic bread.

1 Melt the butter or margarine in a saucepan and add the mushrooms and green onion. Cook over a low heat for 5 minutes. Add the tomatoes and bring to a boil.
2 Stir in the pasta and return to a boil. Simmer for 8–10 minutes, or until the pasta is tender. Spoon into a serving bowl and serve with the grated cheese.

SERVES: *1*
PREPARATION TIME: *5 minutes*
COOKING TIME: *10 minutes*
FREEZING: *not recommended*

INGREDIENTS
1 teaspoon butter or margarine
1 oz button mushrooms, wiped and thinly sliced
1 green onion, trimmed and finely chopped
7 fl oz can of chopped tomatoes with herbs
1 1/2 oz small pasta shapes, e.g. bows, quills, spirals, etc.
1 oz fresh Parmesan cheese, grated

Family meals

*A*s your children grow and learn, family mealtimes can gradually become relaxing and enjoyable occasions for every one. In these busy times, sitting down together may be quite a rare event. Nevertheless, good behavior and table manners should be encouraged from the time your baby is able to sit in the high chair and join you at the dining table. Babies are excellent at mimicry, so the best way for them to learn these social skills is to put them into practice yourself.

Getting children involved

In view of today's busy lifestyle, I have devised the recipes for this final chapter in two sections. The first is for rather special main-course recipes and has been selected with family celebrations in mind. Throughout the year, special events crop up, such as birthdays and anniversaries, or simply that the whole family can manage to eat together at the same time. Children like to be included from a very young age; participating in these events can make them feel very grown-up. At the same time, craftily encourage good eating habits. Whether the meal is to be formal or not, get the children involved wherever practicable. Let them help with designing or writing the invitations, writing the shopping lists, preparing some of the food or helping to set the table. Even the smallest toddler can fold a paper napkin in some fashion. The dishes in this section can be made in advance, so there are no last-minute panics, and there are suggestions for suitable vegetable accompaniments, plus advice on how to adapt them very straightforwardly for the children.

In the second part of the chapter is a selection of recipes that you will probably use more often, for quick suppers. Very often it is the last meal of the day that causes the most consternation to the cook. With a young family to care for, inspiration as well as energy may well be flagging by the evening, which is why I have designed these recipes so that they can be prepared and cooked with the minimum of effort and be on the table in under half an hour.

Special Meals

Throughout the year, special events arise that are a cause for celebration: birthdays, anniversaries or simply the whole family managing to be together at the same time. So what better way to do this than with a sumptuous lunch or dinner?

SERVES: *6–8*
PREPARATION TIME: *1 1/4 hours*
COOKING TIME: *1 hour 20 minutes*
FREEZING: *recommended*

INGREDIENTS
FOR THE FILLING:
2 1/2 cups vegetable stock
1/2 cup each brown rice and wild rice
3 tablespoons olive oil
1 onion, finely chopped
1 celery stalk, finely chopped
4 carrots, grated
1/4 cup chopped fresh cilantro
3 large eggs, beaten
1/2 cup ground hazelnuts, toasted
2 teaspoons ground cumin
1/4 cup grated mature Cheddar cheese
freshly ground black pepper
FOR THE HERB CRUST:
1 1/2 cups each unbleached all-purpose and whole wheat flours
3/4 cup or 1 1/2 sticks butter or margarine
3 tablespoons chopped fresh herbs
5–6 tablespoons milk

Vegetable terrine

This terrine looks spectacular and slices easily. It does require quite lengthy preparation, but this is more than compensated for by the final result. Serve as a main course with stir-fried Brussels sprouts and roasted root vegetables sprinkled with rosemary.

1 Bring the stock to a boil in a large saucepan. Add all the rice and return to a boil. Reduce the heat, cover the pan and let simmer for 20 minutes, or until the rice has absorbed most of the stock. Reduce the heat to very low and cook for a further 5 minutes, stirring occasionally.

2 Meanwhile, heat the olive oil in a frying pan and cook the onion and celery over medium heat for 5 minutes, or until softened. Add the carrots and cook for 3 more minutes.

3 Stir the vegetables into the rice, with the cilantro, two-thirds of the beaten eggs, the hazelnuts, cumin and half the Cheddar cheese. Season with black pepper.

4 Grease and line the bottom of a 2 lb. loaf pan measuring 10 × 5 inches. Preheat the oven to 350°F. Spoon the rice mixture into the pan, pressing it down firmly with the back of a spoon. Cook for 50 minutes, or until firm. Leave to cool in the pan.

5 Meanwhile, make the herb crust. Sift the flours into a bowl with a pinch of salt. Cut in the butter or margarine, until the mixture resembles fine bread crumbs. Stir in the herbs, the remaining Cheddar cheese and enough milk to form a soft, but not sticky, dough. Wrap the dough in plastic wrap and chill until needed.

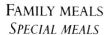
6 Roll out three-quarters of the herb dough on a lightly floured surface to a rectangle large enough to encase the filling. Turn the rice terrine out on to the center of the pastry and peel away the lining paper. Moisten the edges of the pastry, lift them over the terrine and seal the ends together down the center of the filling. Tuck in the end flaps and seal them underneath, like a package. Put the terrine on a baking sheet.

7 Roll out the reserved pastry and cut out pastry leaves of various sizes. Dampen the leaves and arrange them along the center of the pastry, to hide the seams. Chill for 15 minutes. Preheat the oven to 400° F.

8 Use the remaining beaten egg to glaze the pastry completely. Bake the terrine for 40 minutes, or until the pastry is golden and the filling thoroughly heated through. Allow to cool for 10 minutes before slicing.

HINTS AND TIPS
Be sure the hazelnuts are finely ground before serving this to children. For a Christmas decoration, use holly-shaped pastry leaves for decorating.

SERVES: 6
PREPARATION TIME: *45 minutes*
STANDING TIME: *30 minutes*
COOKING TIME: *20 minutes*
FREEZING: *not recommended*

INGREDIENTS
1 eggplant, cut in 1-inch cubes
2 teaspoons salt
6 corn on the cobs
*1 each red, green and yellow pepper,
    seeded and cut in 1-inch squares*
4 zucchini, cut in 6 pieces
24 cherry tomatoes
FOR THE GLAZE:
¼ cup low-sodium soy sauce
1 tablespoon clear honey
1 tablespoon vegetable oil
FOR THE SAUCE:
2 cups natural roasted peanuts
4 tablespoons butter or margarine
1 tablespoon light turbinado sugar
2 teaspoons tahini paste
1 garlic clove, crushed
1 good cup water
*a pinch each of salt and cayenne
    pepper*

Vegetable satay

**Combined with the vegetables, the peanut sauce essential to satays
is a good source of the B vitamins thiamine and niacin, as well as
protein and fiber. Serve at a summer barbecue with mushroom
kebabs and Lightning Burgers (see page 85).**

1 Soak 24 bamboo skewers in hot water. Layer the eggplant cubes
in a colander, with the salt. Let stand for 30 minutes. Rinse well
under cold running water.

2 Remove the husks and silk threads from the corn and cut each
cob in four. Thread all the vegetables and the tomatoes alternately
on to the skewers.

3 Warm the soy sauce, honey and oil in a small saucepan and brush
the mixture over the kebabs to glaze them. Cook the kebabs on the
barbecue or under a preheated broiler for 15 minutes, brushing them
with the remaining glaze and turning them frequently, until the
vegetables are tender.

4 Meanwhile, make the sauce. Chop the peanuts and butter or
margarine in a food processor or blender until smooth. Spoon the
mixture into a saucepan and stir in the sugar, tahini paste, water, salt
and cayenne pepper. Stir over low heat for 5 minutes, or until the
sauce is hot and well amalgamated.

HINTS AND TIPS
*Remove the wooden kebab sticks
before serving this to children.
Make the sauce in advance and store
it in a container in the refrigerator.*

Tomato and onion tart

Ideal for a spring lunch party, this is somewhat similar to a pizza, but the pastry shell gives it a lighter texture. To eat it at its best, serve it as soon as it comes out of the oven. Potato salad and a selection of salad leaves are good accompaniments.

SERVES: 6
PREPARATION TIME: *30 minutes*
CHILLING TIME: *15 minutes*
COOKING TIME: *1 hour*
FREEZING: *recommended, for tart case only*

INGREDIENTS
FOR THE TART CASE:
good 1 1/2 cups unbleached all-purpose white flour
6 tablespoons butter or margarine
1 teaspoon Dijon mustard
1 large egg
FOR THE FILLING:
2 lb onions, thinly sliced
2 garlic cloves, crushed
1/2 cup olive oil
14 oz can of tomatoes
1 tablespoon tomato paste
1 teaspoon sugar
1 teaspoon dried oregano
1 green pepper, seeded and cut in strips
2 oz each black and green olives, pitted
salt and freshly ground black pepper

1 To make the pastry, sift the flour into a bowl and rub in the butter or margarine, until the mixture resembles fine bread crumbs. Beat the mustard and egg together and add them to the bowl, with enough water to form a soft, but not sticky, dough.

2 Roll out the dough on a lightly floured surface to about 1/4-inch thick and use it to line a 10-inch loose-based flan pan. Prick the base and chill it for 15 minutes.

3 Preheat the oven to 400°F. Line the pastry case with wax paper and baking beans and bake it blind for 10 minutes. Remove the paper and beans and bake for 10 minutes more, or until the pastry has set and is very pale golden.

4 For the filling, cook the onions and garlic in 6 tablespoons of olive oil over low heat for 40 minutes, or until the onions are soft and pale golden.

5 Meanwhile, put the tomatoes, tomato paste, sugar and oregano into a clean saucepan and bring to a boil. Boil steadily, stirring occasionally until the mixture is reduced to about 1/2 cup. Stir the tomato mixture into the onions and season well with salt and pepper.

6 Spoon the mixture into the pastry case and level the surface with the back of a spoon. Arrange the pepper strips in a lattice pattern on top and place the olives in alternate spaces. Brush the top with some of the remaining olive oil and bake for 10 minutes.

7 Brush the top with oil again and bake for another 10 minutes, or until the peppers have softened.

SERVES: *6*
PREPARATION TIME: *20 minutes*
COOKING TIME: *30 minutes*
FREEZING: *not recommended*

INGREDIENTS

½ cup peanut oil

1 tablespoon granulated sugar

6 corn on the cobs

*1 each red and green pepper, seeded
and chopped*

2 celery stalks, thickly sliced

1 onion, chopped

1 garlic clove, crushed

¾ cup long-grain brown rice

1¾ cups vegetable stock

*1 lb tomatoes; skinned, seeded and
chopped*

½ teaspoon dried thyme

a pinch of ground allspice

1 pinch of cayenne pepper

*14 oz can of gunga peas, drained
and rinsed*

3 tablespoons chopped fresh parsley

½ cup flaked almonds, toasted

Corn jambalaya

*For an autumn supper party — a hearty rice stew that really needs
no other dish to accompany it, except perhaps some corn muffins
and steamed broccoli. The caramelized corn takes only a few
minutes; keep watching the pan, or the corn will quickly burn.
Gunga peas are like small, round borlotti beans; they are available
in health stores.*

1 Heat the oil and sugar together over low heat until the sugar has
dissolved. Increase the heat and cook until the sugar is a light
caramel. Meanwhile, remove the outer husks and silk threads from
the corn cobs. Cut each in four pieces.

2 Add the corn cobs to the pan and cook them over low heat for
about 8 minutes, turning them frequently to coat them evenly in the
caramel mixture. Remove the pan from the heat, and, using a slotted
spoon, lift the corn cobs out. (You may have to cook the cobs in
batches.)

3 Add the peppers, celery, onion and garlic to the pan. Return the
pan to the heat and cook, stirring occasionally, for 5 minutes, or
until the vegetables have softened. Mix in the rice, stock, tomatoes,
thyme, spices and peas. Bring to a boil.

4 Reduce the heat, cover the pan and leave to cook gently for 20
minutes.

5 Stir in the corn cobs and cook them for another 5–10 minutes, or
until the rice and vegetables are tender. Sprinkle over the parsley
and almonds just before you serve.

HINTS AND TIPS
*Provide plenty of napkins so your
guests can wipe their sticky fingers
after eating the corn cobs.*

QUICK SUPPERS

To me, super-quick recipes should be as the description says: super meals you can prepare and cook in under 30 minutes. No one wants to spend hours cooking during a weekday evening, but you still want to feed your family well. In this section there is over a week's worth of recipes and ideas to enable you to achieve just that.

No-crust quiche

Often the most tricky part of a quiche is the pastry, so why not skip it and cook just the filling? It's a great way to use up cooked, leftover vegetables and pulses; the variations are endless, though here is a popular favorite. Serve with baked beans and crusty bread.

1 Preheat the oven to 375°F. Lightly grease a 7-inch quiche dish. Heat the oil in a small pan and fry the onion and garlic for 5 minutes, until golden. Spoon the onion into the base of the dish and sprinkle the cheese on top.
2 Beat together the eggs, cream and nutmeg. Season well with salt and pepper. Strain the eggs over the cheese mixture in the dish and arrange the tomato slices on top.
3 Bake for 25 minutes, or until the mixture is set and the top golden.

SERVES: *4*
PREPARATION TIME: *10 minutes*
COOKING TIME: *20 minutes*
FREEZING: *not recommended*

INGREDIENTS
1 tablespoon olive oil
1 large onion, finely sliced
1 garlic clove, crushed
1½ cups grated Cheddar cheese
3 large eggs, beaten
1¼ cups light cream or half-and-half
a pinch of grated nutmeg
2 firm tomatoes, sliced
salt and freshly ground black pepper

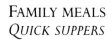

Alpine fondue

A great supper dish to make, even if you don't have a fondue set. It is fairly high in fat, so offset this by providing a selection of raw crunchy vegetables for dipping in. Serve with cubes of crusty bread, cauliflower flowerets, sliced carrots, button mushrooms, baby corn cobs and seeded and chopped sweet peppers.

SERVES: *4–6*
PREPARATION TIME: *10 minutes*
COOKING TIME: *15 minutes*
FREEZING: *not recommended*

INGREDIENTS
1 garlic clove, crushed
1 1/4 cups dry white wine or white grape juice
juice of 1/2 small lemon
1 1/2 cup grated Emmenthal cheese
1 cup grated Gruyère cheese
2 teaspoons cornstarch
1/4 cup water
salt and freshly ground black pepper

1 Put the garlic, wine and lemon juice in a large, heavy-based saucepan. Stir in the cheeses. Stir over low heat until all the cheese has melted.

2 Blend the cornstarch with the water to form a smooth paste. Stir the paste into the melted cheese and cook over medium heat, until it has thickened and is smooth.

3 Season with salt and pepper and serve at once, dipping the bread and vegetables into the cheese.

HINTS AND TIPS
Children love dipping into fondues, but the cheese can be dangerously hot; for safety, provide younger children with their very own dish of fondue mixture set on a dinner plate.

Country-style eggs

This is a meat-free version of the classic recipe for scotch eggs. High in fiber and protein, country-style eggs make a satisfying supper, with coleslaw, steamed corn and tomatoes; or serve them cold in a lunch box.

1 Make up the stuffing with boiling water according to the package instructions. Divide the mixture into quarters and roll out one quarter on a lightly floured surface, to a 5–6-inch circle. Dampen the edges and wrap it around a hard-boiled egg, to seal the egg in completely. Repeat with the remaining stuffing and eggs.
2 Beat the egg on a plate, and mix together the bread crumbs and pumpkin seeds on a second plate. Coat each stuffing-coated egg in egg first, and then in the bread crumb mixture.
3 Heat the oil in a deep saucepan, until the temperature reaches 375° F, or when a cube of bread rises and sizzles within 30 seconds. Deep-fry the eggs for 8–10 minutes over medium-low heat, until they are crisp and golden. Drain them on paper towels.

SERVES: *4*
PREPARATION TIME: *20 minutes*
COOKING TIME: *10 minutes*
FREEZING: *not recommended*

INGREDIENTS
1 package of country-style stuffing mix
4 tablespoons unbleached all-purpose flour
4 large hard-boiled eggs, shelled
1 large egg
2 cups fresh whole wheat bread crumbs
2 heaping tablespoons pumpkin seeds, roughly crushed
corn oil for deep-frying

French onion soup

A rich, satisfying winter soup that makes the most of simple cupboard ingredients. Use sweet yellow or Spanish onions, if they're available.

1 Melt the butter or margarine in a saucepan. Add the onions and sugar and cook the onions over medium–high heat, stirring occasionally, for 10 minutes or until they are a deep golden brown.
2 Remove the pan from the heat and stir in the flour. Gradually stir in the stock. Add the bay leaf and season with salt and pepper. Stir the soup over medium heat until it has thickened slightly. Cover the pan and leave the soup to simmer for about 20 minutes.
3 Meanwhile, toast the bread on one side. Sprinkle the cheese on the untoasted side and broil until the cheese is golden and bubbling. Ladle the soup into bowls and float a slice of bread on top.

SERVES: *4*
PREPARATION TIME: *5 minutes*
COOKING TIME: *25 minutes*
FREEZING: *not recommended*

INGREDIENTS
4 tablespoons butter or margarine
2 onions, sliced
1/2 teaspoon dark turbinado sugar
3 tablespoons unbleached all-purpose flour
3 3/4 cups vegetable stock
1 bay leaf
salt and freshly ground black pepper
TO SERVE:
4 slices of French bread
3/4 cup grated Gruyère, Cheddar or Colby cheese

INGREDIENTS

1 tablespoon olive oil

3 green onions, chopped

1 lb tomatoes, skinned and roughly chopped

1 tablespoon tomato paste

a pinch of dried basil

8 oz polenta meal

3 oz crumbly cheese, e.g. Cheddar or Monterey Jack

salt and freshly ground black pepper

Polenta with cheese

Polenta or cornmeal is a great source of energy and vitamins. It is high in carbohydrate and cooks to a smooth, creamy porridge, rather like mashed potatoes. Serve this polenta bake with steamed green beans or a mixed-leaf salad.

1 Heat the oil in a saucepan and add the green onions, tomatoes, tomato paste and basil. Season lightly with salt and pepper and bring to a boil. Allow to simmer over a low heat, uncovered, until the mixture has thickened slightly.

2 Meanwhile, bring 4¼ cups of unsalted water to a boil. Add the polenta meal in a slow, steady stream, stirring continuously. Stir the polenta over low heat, and, as it begins to thicken, beat the polenta vigorously until it begins to pull away from the sides of the pan.

3 Quickly spoon the polenta into a lightly oiled, shallow, flameproof dish. Make a well in the center and pour in the tomato mixture. Crumble the cheese on top of the tomatoes and broil until golden.

INGREDIENTS

1 oz dried mixed mushrooms, e.g. ceps, chanterelles or morels

1 tablespoon olive oil

1 red onion, sliced

1 garlic clove, crushed

8 oz button mushrooms, quartered

1 good cup arborio, risotto or round-grain pudding rice

4¼ cups vegetable stock

¼ cup chopped fresh parsley

salt and freshly ground black pepper

¼ cup fresh grated parmesan cheese, to serve

Forest-mushroom risotto

Dried mushrooms are a great standby. Their flavor is more intense than fresh mushrooms, so only a few are needed. Remember to soak them in the morning, ready for supper.

1 Put the mushrooms in a small bowl and pour over enough boiling water to cover them by about ½ inch. Leave to soak for at least 30 minutes.

2 Drain the soaked mushrooms and chop them roughly. Heat the oil in a large saucepan and cook the onion and garlic until softened. Stir in all the mushrooms and rice and half the stock. Bring the stock to a boil.

3 Cook the risotto over medium heat, stirring frequently, until all the stock has been absorbed. Stir in the remaining stock and continue cooking, stirring occasionally, until the rice is tender and all the stock has been absorbed.

4 Stir in the parsley. Season the risotto with salt and pepper and spoon it into warm bowls. Sprinkle over the parmesan cheese just before you serve.

Three-pepper pizza

To save time, use a ready-prepared pizza dough or the toasted halves of a flat country-style loaf that has been sliced lengthwise; if you've planned ahead, make the pizza dough in advance. Serve with cucumber sticks and wedges of baby lettuce.

1 Heat half the oil in a large frying pan and cook the pepper rings over medium heat until they are softened. Remove them with a slotted spoon.

2 Heat the remaining oil in the pan and add the onion, garlic, tomatoes and tomato paste and bring to a boil. Reduce the heat and leave to simmer for 5 minutes. Preheat the oven to 400° F.

3 Put the pizza dough on a baking sheet and spoon the tomato mixture over it. Arrange the pepper rings and mozzarella slices on top and then sprinkle over the oregano. Cook for 20 minutes, or until the cheese is bubbling.

Serves: *4*
Preparation time: *10 minutes*
Cooking time: *20 minutes*
Freezing: *not recommended*

Ingredients
3 tablespoons olive oil
1 each red, green and yellow peppers, seeded and sliced in rings
1 red onion, sliced
1 garlic clove, crushed
14 oz can of chopped tomatoes with herbs
1 tablespoon tomato paste
10-inch pizza base
4 oz mozzarella cheese, sliced
1/2 teaspoon dried oregano

Hints and tips
Make mini-pizzas for children, using English muffin halves for the dough.

Glossary of terms

Glossary

Agar flakes/powder Setting, thickening and gelling agent made from seaweed. Rich in iron and other minerals and has no flavor, so it is suitable for sweet and savory dishes.

Arrowroot powder Derived from the root of the plant. Used to make thin, clear sauces and glazes. In health food shops, sometimes sold under the Japanese title "kuzu".

Bean sprouts Sprouting shoots from seeds or pulses: most commonly available type is mung bean sprouts. Easy to prepare at home.

Blanch Cook briefly in boiling water for a few minutes.

Bulgur Kernels of wheat that have been cooked, dried and cracked. Finely cracked grains require no cooking, only soaking in boiling water or stock. Cook larger grains like rice.

Carob bars/powder Made from roasted, ground seedpods of locust tree. Naturally sweet, it tastes similar to chocolate.

Caramelize Turn sugar into caramel by heating it gently until it turns golden brown. Some vegetables can be caramelized by cooking them in sugar, water and butter to produce a light golden glaze.

Charlotte Molded dish set in round pan or ramekin.

Cornmeal Sometimes called maize meal or polenta; finely ground golden grain extracted from whole corn kernels. Cooked polenta is soft and porridge-like, and can be further baked, roasted or fried. Also used in baking.

Creamed coconut Solidified extract of coconut; can be crumbled directly into stews or dissolved in boiling water. Used in both sweet and savory dishes.

Garam masala Basic ground curry powder.

Garbanzo beans Hard, cream-colored pulse; can be bought dried or canned. Used in salads and stews, or ground to make flour (gram flour). Mashed, it is the main ingredient in hummus.

Glaze Make baked food look glossy or brown by brushing with milk or beaten egg before cooking.

Gluten Protein found in grains such as wheat. When mixed with liquid, produces elasticity in dough and helps it rise.

Hull Remove stalks and core or calyx from soft fruit, such as strawberries.

Kilocalorie Measurement of energy value of foods.

Marinate Soak food in liquid to add flavor and, sometimes, improve tenderness.

Poach Cook food in very gently simmering liquid.

Poppy seeds Tiny black seeds used in salads, baking and as garnish. Good source of protein.

Purée Blend and/or strain food until smooth.

Reduce Concentrate or thicken liquid by rapid boiling.

Risotto Savory dish of rice and vegetables.

Sesame seeds Small, pearly, pale seeds add nutty flavor when toasted and used in toppings, coatings, etc. Pungent oil from ground roasted seeds used in Chinese recipes.

Skim Remove froth or scum from surface of boiling liquid.

Soya flour High-protein, gluten-free baking and thickening agent, made from ground soya beans.

Soya milk Soya beans soaked, ground and filtered to produce milk.

Soy sauce Fermented soya beans used as a condiment and flavoring in savory dishes, especially Chinese and Far-Eastern cooking. Look out for the low-sodium brands and avoid those containing monosodium glutamate, a worthless chemical flavor enhancer.

Stir-fry Fry evenly-sized ingredients at high temperature in wok or large frying pan, stirring continually.

Tahini Sesame seed paste.

Tofu Japanese word for soya-bean curd. Bland, almost tasteless food that looks like soft white cheese and is extremely high in protein. Can be bought as soft and crumbly *silken tofu, firm tofu* and *smoked tofu*, which slices like cheese.

Whole foods Grains, pulses, seeds, berries, etc. that have not been treated chemically or refined.

Whole wheat or whole meal Milled flour that still contains the components of the whole grain: bran, germ and gluten.

Yeast Fungus cells used to produce fermentation and cause dough to rise.

Yeast extract Savory spread or seasoning, fortified with B-group vitamins and folic acid. Liquid from yeast, evaporated and mixed with vegetable extract and salt.

Useful basic recipes

Pasta The subject of pasta could be a book in itself; there are endless varieties and shapes. However, the basic recipe couldn't be easier. A pasta machine helps take the hard work out of rolling the prepared dough.

This recipe makes about 12 oz.

INGREDIENTS
2 good cups strong durum wheat flour
2 large eggs
3 tablespoons olive oil
semolina or farina for sprinkling

1 Sift the flour into a bowl. Make a well in the center. Beat together the eggs and oil then add to the flour. Mix gently to form a soft dough.
2 Knead pasta dough on a lightly floured surface for 5 minutes or until silky smooth. Halve the dough and roll out each piece to a 16 x 13 inch rectangle. Trim edges, then cut into even sheets for cannelloni or lasagne.

To make pasta strands:
Roll out two rectangles as before. Sprinkle each lightly with semolina, then roll up each piece loosely like a jelly roll. Using a very sharp knife cut into even strips, immediately unroll strands and place on a baking sheet sprinkled with semolina to prevent sticking.

White pouring sauce (béchamel sauce) Savory white sauce forms the basis to many dishes. Once you have mastered the basic technique the varieties are endless.

This recipe makes about 1¼ pint.

INGREDIENTS
2½ cups milk
1 bouquet garni
pinch fresh grated nutmeg
2 tablespoons butter or margarine
4 tablespoons flour
salt and freshly ground black pepper

1 Put the milk into a saucepan with the bouquet garni and nutmeg. Heat gently until almost boiling, then remove from the heat. Cover and leave to steep for at least 2 hours.
2 Melt butter in a clean saucepan, then remove from the heat and stir in the flour. Cook over low heat for 1 minute. Strain milk. Remove the pan from the heat and gradually add the milk a little at a time, stirring well between each addition.
3 Stir the sauce over a medium heat for 3–4 minutes or until the sauce thickens and is smooth. Simmer very gently for another 4–5 minutes, stirring occasionally. Season with salt and pepper.

Variations:

Herb sauce – Stir in ¼ cup fresh chopped herbs, e.g. parsley, chervil, sage or chives at step 3.

Cheese sauce – Stir in ½ cup grated or crumbled cheese at step 3, with a pinch of dried mustard.

137

Vegetable stock A good, homemade stock can be the base for a great many vegetarian recipes. Commercial brands are available but beware, they often contain generous quantities of salt and sugar, which are unsuitable for babies. Vegetable stock will keep for up to five days in the refrigerator. If you want to freeze the stock, pour it into ice-cube trays or plastic containers. Use frozen.

The recipe given here makes about 4¼ cups.

INGREDIENTS
1 small onion
1 carrot
1 celery stalk
4 oz turnip
4 oz parsnip
4 oz rutabaga
1 oz fresh ginger-root
1 sprig of fresh parsley
1 bay leaf
2 cloves
6 black peppercorns
about 2½ pints cold water

1 Chop all the vegetables and ginger coarsely. Put them in a saucepan, with the herbs and spices. Add the water and bring it slowly to a boil.
2 Cover the pan and simmer gently for about 2 hours, stirring occasionally. Remove from the heat and allow to cool. Strain through a fine strainer and discard the flavorings. Pour the stock into a large jug, cover it and chill until required.

Tomato sauce Commercial brands cannot compete with this delicious homemade variety. Low in fat, salt and sugar, it can be used in a variety of ways. The sauce can be left chunky, and can be frozen for up to 6 months.

This recipe makes 2½ cups.

INGREDIENTS
1 tablespoon olive oil
1 medium onion, peeled and finely chopped
1 garlic clove, crushed
1 teaspoon each chopped fresh thyme, oregano and parsley
1 lb ripe tomatoes, skinned, deseeded and chopped
14 oz can Italian peeled tomatoes
freshly ground black pepper

1 Heat the oil in a large saucepan. Add the onion and garlic and cook over medium heat for 10 minutes, stirring occasionally.
2 Add the herbs, fresh tomatoes, canned tomatoes and their juice. Bring to a boil, reduce heat, partially cover the pan and simmer for 45–50 minutes, stirring occasionally.
3 Season sauce well with pepper, cool slightly then liquidize to a smooth consistency. Store in a sealed container in the refrigerator for up to 3 days.

Tomato paste Concentrated tomato paste adds flavor and color to soups and stews. Make this during the summer when fresh tomatoes are at their best, both in quality and price.

This recipe makes about 1¾ cups.

INGREDIENTS
3 lb fresh ripe tomatoes
pinch salt and sugar

1 Wash and roughly chop the tomatoes. Put into a large saucepan and cook over a medium heat until softened. Bring to a boil, reduce heat, cover and simmer for 20 minutes, stirring occasionally.
2 Cool slightly, then purée in a food processor or blender. Pass paste through a nylon strainer into a saucepan to remove seeds. Add salt and sugar, then bring paste to the boil, reduce heat and simmer very gently, stirring occasionally, for about 1½–1¾ hours, or until mixture becomes so thick, it will remain in two halves when a wooden spoon is drawn through the center.
3 Allow mixture to cool then spoon into an airtight container and store in refrigerator for up to 1 month.

To freeze:
Freeze in ice cube trays, then turn out frozen cubes and store in plastic bags for up to 8 months.

Fruit tea bread Teabreads are usually enriched with fruit and served sliced, spread with butter or margarine. Many places have their own traditional recipe but this is one I make time after time. It is just as good for breakfast or in a packed lunch as it is served with tea or coffee. The loaves can be frozen.

This recipe makes 1 loaf.

INGREDIENTS

1 cup each golden raisins and currants
1 cup dark brown sugar
1 orange, grated zest and juice
1 ¼ cups strong hot tea
good 2 ½ cups self-rising whole wheat flour
1 large egg, beaten

1 Put the fruit into a large bowl and stir in the sugar, orange zest and juice, then pour in the hot tea. Cover and leave to soak overnight.
2 Preheat the oven at 300° F. Grease and line the base of a 2 lb loaf pan. Sift the flour into the fruit, adding any bran left in the sifter. Beat in the egg, then spoon mixture into loaf pan. Level the surface and bake for 1½– 1¾ hours, or until a toothpick inserted into the center comes out clean.
3 Allow the tea bread to cool in the pan for about 20 minutes, then turn out and cool on a wire rack. Store in an airtight pan.

Whole wheat bread Bread has been one of the main staples of the world for centuries. Most bread is made with yeast; the dough is kneaded, shaped and allowed to rise. Breads that contain no yeast such as naan or bagels are called unleavened. Fresh yeast can be bought at independent bakers or health food stores and any not used can be frozen. The bread dough and the cooked loaves can also be frozen.

This recipe makes 2 loaves.

INGREDIENTS

1 ½ oz fresh yeast
3 ¾ cups tepid water
3 lb strong whole wheat flour
2 teaspoons superfine sugar
4 teaspoons salt
2 tablespoons margarine

1 Mix the yeast with about 1 ¼ cups of the water until dissolved. Mix the flour, sugar and salt in a large bowl. Cut in the margarine then make a well in the center and add the yeast and enough of the remaining water to form a soft slightly sticky dough.
2 Knead the dough on a lightly floured surface for 10 minutes or until it is smooth, soft and elastic. Put it in a clean bowl, cover with greased plastic wrap and leave in a warm place for about 1 hour or until dough has doubled in size.
3 Turn out and knead again for 10 minutes. Grease two 2 lb loaf pans. Halve the dough and knead each half again until smooth, then shape to fit the pans. Put dough in pans and cover with greased plastic wrap. Leave in a warm place until dough reduces the top rim of each pan.
4 Set the oven at 450° F. Uncover dough, brush tops with milk and bake in center of oven for 35–40 minutes or until the base of each loaf sounds hollow when tapped. Cool on a wire rack.
To make rolls: Divide dough into 2 oz pieces and shape into rounds, or ovals. Bake for 15–20 minutes.

Beans, pulses, peas and lentils

Beans and pulses All dried beans and most pulses need to be soaked, so they absorb water and return to their natural size. Soaking doubles the weight of dried beans, so when a recipe calls for 8 oz of cooked beans you need to soak 4 oz.

Spread the beans out in a single layer on a plate and discard any discolored ones or pieces of grit. Rinse the beans in a colander until the water runs clear and then put them into a bowl large enough to allow the beans to expand. There are two methods of soaking: hot-soaking and cold-soaking. Hot-soaking is the quickest: most beans will have absorbed the maximum amount of water within about 2 hours. Cold-soaking needs at least 6 hours and most recipes recommend cold-soaking overnight. Whatever method you choose, pour over enough boiling or cold water to cover the beans by at least 4 inches.

Drain the soaked beans and put them in a large saucepan. Cover with fresh, cold water and bring to a boil. Do not add salt; added salt is harmful to youngsters and will toughen the beans. Boil briskly, uncovered, for 10 minutes; this is essential for all beans, to rid them of toxic substances that can upset the digestive system. Reduce the heat, skim the surface to remove froth, partially cover the pan with a lid and simmer for about an hour.

Peas and lentils Whole peas and garbanzo beans need to be soaked and cooked in the same way as beans and pulses. Split-peas and lentils do not need soaking or pre-cooking: add them to your recipe and cook for 30–40 minutes, or until tender.

Put the peas and lentils on a plate and pick out the grit and any discolored ones. Rinse them in a colander or strainer.

To cook them on their own, not as an ingredient in a recipe, put them into a saucepan and cover them with unsalted water or vegetable stock. Allow about 3¾ pints of liquid for every 4 oz. Bring the liquid to a boil, skim the surface to remove any froth, and then partially cover the pan and simmer gently for ¾–1 hour for split-peas, 20 minutes for red lentils and 30–35 minutes for green or brown lentils.

Sprouting beans, peas and seeds

Home-sprouting is easily done and doesn't need much equipment or storage space. A wide-necked jam jar, a piece of clean cheesecloth or absorbent wiper, and a rubber band are all you need. Bean sprouts are highly nutritious, being very rich in protein, fiber, vitamins, minerals and starch. Children love growing their own sprouts, and, as the germination time is fairly short (3–6 days, depending on the type) the fruits of their labors can soon be seen.

Use beans that are intended for eating or sprouting and not ones intended for planting, which may have been treated with a preservative. Choose any of the following: aduki beans, garbanzo beans, lentils, mung beans or soya beans. Soak soya beans for a couple of hours to soften the outer husks. Seeds to try sprouting are alfalfa, poppy, sesame, sunflower or pumpkin seeds, or whole grains such as wheat.

Three steps to sprouting success

1 Soak or rinse the seed or beans and put them in a large, wide-necked jam jar, with 1–2 tablespoons of water. Cover the jar with cheesecloth and secure it with a rubber band. Store out of the light at a constant room temperature. **2** Every day, pour cold water into the jar through the cheesecloth. Drain off excess water, shaking the beans gently as you do so. Leave the jar upside-down for a few minutes, to drain off the last drops of water. Replace out of the light. Don't let the beans sit in water, or they will rot. **3** The bean sprouts are ready for harvesting when the shoots are about 1 inch long. Put them in a strainer and rinse them well with cold water.

Index

Credits

*Quarto would like to thank the
following for permission to
reproduce copyright material.*
*p.6: M. Tcherevkoff/Image Bank;
p.16: Pictor; p.36: Terry Williams/
Image Bank; p.68: Jeff Robins/Ace;
p.70: Mark French/Ace; p.124: Juan
Silva/Image Bank.*
*All other photographs are copyright of
Quarto Inc.*

14.99